OXFORDSHIRE

Edited by Lynsey Hawkins

First published in Great Britain in 2003 by
YOUNG WRITERS
Remus House,
Coltsfoot Drive,
Peterborough, PE2 9JX
Telephone (01733) 890066

HB ISBN 1 84460 113 7
SB ISBN 1 84460 112 9

FOREWORD

Young Writers was established in 1991 as a foundation for promoting the reading and writing of poetry amongst children and young adults. Today it continues this quest and proceeds to nurture and guide the writing talents of today's youth.

From this year's competition Young Writers is proud to present a showcase of the best poetic talent from across the UK. Each hand-picked poem has been carefully chosen from over 66,000 'Hullabaloo!' entries to be published in this, our eleventh primary school series.

This year in particular we have been wholeheartedly impressed with the quality of entries received. The thought, effort, imagination and hard work put into each poem impressed us all and once again the task of editing was a difficult but enjoyable experience.

We hope you are as pleased as we are with the final selection and that you and your family will continue to be entertained with *Hullabaloo! Oxfordshire* for many years to come.

CONTENTS

The Poems

New York, New York

It's the city that never sleeps,
Yellow cabs fill the streets,
The people pour in to get to work,
In the shadows the muggers lurk,
In the day people see the sights
And is bright in the nights,
Central Park is the place to go,
Times Square is where you see a show.
The Chrysler Building with its gleaming spire,
Only the Empire State is higher,
The World Trade Center is no more,
NYPD control the law,
Go to New York for a holiday,
You might end up wanting to stay.

Charlie Rodgers (11)
All Saints CE (A) Primary School

You Horrible Girl!

You never tidy your room
(Oh come on I use the broom)
What happened to your schoolwork?
(I don't know, that's for jerks!)
You don't even have any friends
(Well they drive me round the bend)
Why don't you like me?
(I can't believe you can't see!)

Amy Killinger (10)
All Saints CE (A) Primary School

SEASONS

Snow falls silently on the garden path,
Children giggle, as stories are told,
The first snowdrop appears.

Here comes spring, flowers sprout,
Lots of babies born, children scream and shout,
While watching daffodils grow.

Days get hotter, hot, hot, hot,
Summer's here, blackbirds sing, church bells ring,
Splash, splosh, children play,
Holidays here, there and everywhere.

Days cool down,
Autumn's here, leaves and wind whip your face
And hair is blown about.

Winter's here again.

Becca Hart (10)
All Saints CE (A) Primary School

AN OWL POEM

A bird's mum has gone to fly
Has gone to find a pie
Comes back with worms
With lots of mud germs
Then they watch the evening sky.

Her wings are white
She flies at night
They are surrounded by sand
At the end of a hot land
She opens her eyelids at midnight.

Her mum pats her beak
When she plays hide-and-seek
She goes to bed at dawn
When she starts to yawn
She sleeps through the shining sun.

Katy Manthorpe (8)
All Saints CE (A) Primary School

THE RACE IN SPACE

I saw an alien in space,
Flying in a race,
I saw some bits of junk
And built a flying skunk,
I joined the alien in the race
And flew at an exceeding pace,
I passed lots of glittering stars,
I even saw the planet Mars
And when I'd crossed the finish line,
The trophy was mine, mine, mine,
I went down and down,
To my home town,
My brother Marty,
Set up a party,
My mum just had to make
Some of her wonderful cake,
At the end of the day,
I was happy to lay,
Down on my bed,
To snuggle my ted.

Bethany Moffett (10)
All Saints CE (A) Primary School

First Day At School

You walk into the playground
Lots of children playing
You go into the cloakroom
Then to your new class.
You can see the teacher
Telling children off
You could make lots of friends today
You might get lots of bullies.
You might get very hard work
It could be easy too.
You get shown round the school
Talking to your friends
It's very nearly lunchtime
You've just ended maths.
You wait for your sandwiches
And talk to the lunchtime helpers
Now it's time for lunch.
You're looking for a place to sit
Your friends all had school dinners
When you've finished, out you go
And then we all go in.
You do lots of work
Now you're very tired
Nearly the end of the day
You watch the clock go round
At last it's time to go.

Samuel Bamford (8)
All Saints CE (A) Primary School

SOMETHING ELSE

S trange
O dd
M ean
E nvy
T alentless
H orrible
I gnore
N asty
G laring

E mbarrassed
L onely
S taring
E nemy.

Sarah Moffat (11)
All Saints CE (A) Primary School

BILLY

(An ode to my late hamster)

It's not the same without Billy,
No more nibbling grapes,
No more chewing the cage bars,
No more escaping from his amazing cage,
No more noisy bedtimes,
No more licks of his clean water,
No more noisy chews of his scrummy food
And no more biting my finger!

Edward Bird (9)
Aston & Cote CE Primary School

FOOTBALLERS

Footballers are cool
And always drool
And footballers rule.
Footballers train every day
And then they start to play.
Footballers earn a lot of money
And sometimes need a dummy.
Footballers are strong and fast
And a long time they last
And mainly like to play
In the good weather forecast.

Footballers get more money than a doctor
And has a shocker.
Some footballers are famous
And sometimes are painless and gameless.
Sometimes they're on the news
And need new shoes
And sometimes get confused.
Footballers care about their fans
And like Stella in their cans.

Footballers control the ball
And some are very tall.
Footballers have very strong kicks
And don't like ticks.
Footballers are good at tackling
And dogs they are always kindly patting.
Footballers love their football,
Footballers are very good at playing football
And some are called Paul.
That's why I like footballers
And I want to be a footballer!

Chloe Payne (9)
Aston & Cote CE Primary School

SHOUTING DISEASE

My mum has a terrible disease
Screaming, shouting, 'Get rid of those fleas!'
Ranting, raving, making Dad start shaving
I think my mum's a shout-a-holic
Screaming to Dad, 'Give up being an alcoholic!'
It's a bad example for the kids
Especially for little Sid
Mum can you stop shouting?
Of course I know it's time for scouting
So will you please stop shouting.
'Tidy your room!'
'Get out the broom!'
'Get in the bath!'
'Wear a scarf!'
Most famous of all,
'Be quiet, I'm making a telephone call!'

Elliot Bradley (9)
Aston & Cote CE Primary School

MEET MY FAMILY

Today when I get home from school
I bet you I will see . . .
My mum talking over the telephone laughing over me,
My brother's fighting over a stupid PlayStation
And my dad's sitting at the table saying we need a vacation.
I really think that I am the only one who's normal
And truthfully from my own small heart
I would rather stay at school!

Jessica Foye (9)
Aston & Cote CE Primary School

THE THRUSH

T he thrush's sweet song carried on the breeze,
H e sits by the nest in the evergreen trees
R eady to take flight
U nder the sunrise light
S preading his wings
H ow many secrets will he sing?

Sarah Weston (8)
Aston & Cote CE Primary School

THERE WAS A COOL PLAYER FROM READING

There was a cool player from Reading
Who went to a match he was dreading
He played like Paul Scholes
And scored loads of goals
Which he did by his wonderful heading!

Franklin Johnson (9)
Aston & Cote CE Primary School

MY LIFE

When I was a baby
Just one year old
I remember the summers boiling hot
And the winters freezing cold.

When I was a toddler
Just about three years old
I remember my cousins
To me they were so big and bold.

When I was a little girl
And I used to have a lunchtime sleep
I used to worship my big sister
But now . . .
She's just a creep!

Charlotte Brooker (9)
Aston & Cote CE Primary School

MY GRANNY'S BEEN TO MARS

My granny's been to Mars
Not the chocolate bar
The *real* Mars.

She made herself a rocket pack
And safety things too.

Next minute, 10, 9, 8, 7, 6, 5, 4, 3, 2, 1, blast-off!
She zoomed up into space
She zoomed all around.

She came back down
Without a frown
On her wrinkled face.
'Guess what?' she cried,
'I won the rocket race!'

She bounced around for the rest of her life
Happy and joyful, isn't that nice?

So if you ever see a granny,
Bouncing all around
I can assure you it will probably be . . .
My gran!

Emily Ross (8)
Aston & Cote CE Primary School

I Know I'm Safe Inside

When the rain is hailing
And the wind is sailing,
I know I'm safe inside.

When the hurricanes are whirling
And the tornadoes are hurling,
I know I'm safe inside.

When the windows are shattering
And the door is clattering
I know I'm safe inside.

At least I think so!

Zara Herring (9)
Aston & Cote CE Primary School

The Sea

Dolphins dive into the sea and waves *splash* on shore
Crabs jump out of shells and snap their enemies.
Coral waves about on the rocks, it's an underwater fantasy
Fish swimming around and octopuses spraying ink around.
It's much better down here than up there on the sand.
I wish I was a fish swimming around
I would see porpoises and electric eels
They would electric themselves around
And manta rays would flap
But now I must return to the noisy world, alas.

Anna Moss (8)
Aston & Cote CE Primary School

Ghost Horse

Every stormy night
When the moon is bright
I can see him in the mist
Trotting up and down
Swiftly turning around
It's the ghost horse
When the ships are tossed at sea
Why does he hide beneath the trees?
When the wind is high, and nobody is passing by
The first signs of dawn begin to show
And then he realises it's time to go.

Anneliese Whiteley (9)
Aston & Cote CE Primary School

Sport Is Cool

Sport is cool,
You silly fool,
You're playing out
And running about,
Football is great,
The pitch is so straight,
Cricket is good,
The bats are wood,
Tennis is fun - in the sun,
In swimming you get . . .
Very wet!

George Windscheffel (9)
Aston & Cote CE Primary School

GUESS IT

Which animal has stripes?
Which animal has pipes?
Which animal is black?
Which animal has a pack?
Which animal is also orange?
Which animal likes eating oranges?

Which animal has sharp claws?
Which animal has furry paws?
Which animal is very furry?
Which animal is very purry?'
Which animal has a long tail?
Which animal is sometimes pale?

A Tiger.

Michael Owen (9)
Aston & Cote CE Primary School

THE STORM

Without a warning a snake of doom
Swirling around in the air
Thrashing thunder striking down
Mountains high calling your name
Rattling lightning, a chain of teeth
A lake roaring like a wild animal
The moon comes out dark not light.

Richard Musgrave (8)
Aston & Cote CE Primary School

As It Came

As I looked through the trees,
I saw an image looking at me,
It had a mane long and silky,
The colour of it was pretty milky,
As it walked up closer to me,
Its beauty blinded all of me,
Between its eyes was a long, pearly horn,
It came to a halt right in front of me,
I opened my mouth,
But the words wouldn't come out,
I was speechless also with its beauty,
It was like there was a curse upon me,
Taking my sight and voice from me,
But what is that beautiful creature?

Phoebe Benfield (8)
Batt CE Primary School

All Alone

Here I stand as still as can be
Nobody's noticed me
I stand and stare all day long
Birds sing and bells ring
But I don't move a limb
I just stand and grow older
And the weather gets colder
Nobody cares what happens to me
I am just a little old tree.

Michelle Moore (11)
Batt CE Primary School

Star Poem

I'm weightless throughout the silent night,
As I glitter and gleam my stunning light,
With my golden shine
And my zig-zaggy lines
The life of a star is unique and fine.

The night has come, the children sleep
And quietly I take a peep,
Though as they share without a care,
Their memories and wishes
I'll be there.

As the sun comes up and I go down,
I slumber deep without a frown,
I dream of the children's wishes to be,
To travel the world, to sail the seas.

And while the moon is there,
Without a care,
I'll glitter throughout the night,
Through the years to come,
I'll be the one,
To shimmer my magical light!

Hettie Dunkley (11)
Batt CE Primary School

The Moon

The moon has a face
Which is silver all over,
It sparkles like diamonds
Like stars in the sky.

Stephanie Fudge (11)
Batt CE Primary School

Me Bedroom!

Me bedroom is horrid,
Me bedroom is pink,
Me bedroom is dirty,
Me bedroom is smelly!

Me bedroom!

Don't go in it, you'll just come back out,
Don't go in it, you'll smell forever,
Don't go in it, it is such a mess,
Don't go in it, everything is on the floor!

Me bedroom!

Me bedroom is horrid,
Me bedroom is pink,
Me bedroom is dirty,
Me bedroom is smelly!

Me bedroom! Keep out!

Lauren Hughes (10)
Batt CE Primary School

Flowers

Flowers, flowers lovely and bright
I could sit and watch them day and night.
Smell the scent of the fully grown flowers
Now the flowers need a shower of water.
Now the flower has gone
Had its happy days
Now it's gone
We can grow more.

Jessica Cox & Mabel Appleton (7)
Batt CE Primary School

THE RAIN

The rain splatters gently to the ground
It makes a *tip-tap tappy* sound.
It splashes on the garden
It waters all the flowers
It fills up all puddles
And it lasts for hours and hours.

Children outside in their wellies,
They put up their umbrellas to play,
While mums and dads
They stay inside
To gaze only the day away.

I love the rain
It's cold and fresh
It makes me feel alive
But it's the magic of the rain
When it mixes with the sun
It's always amazing and wonderful
When at last . . .
A rainbow has come.

Luke Hosegood (7)
Batt CE Primary School

BORING, BORING HOMEWORK

Boring, boring homework, times tables all that stuff.
All last week's spellings were wrong,
So the teacher got all in a huff.

Boring, boring homework, writing stories all on your own.
Wanting help from Mum
But she's still chatting on the phone.

Boring, boring homework, now my arm is aching.
I'd rather go out with my sister
Or help Mum with the baking.

Boring, boring homework, wanting to go out and play.
I'll put it in my book bag
And do it another day!

Luisa Smith (7)
Batt CE Primary School

My Family

Harry the youngest of the family
He goes to nursery still.
But poor old Dad
On Saturday was ill.

But getting back to Callum
He's a funny old chap.
I like a bit of
Tipperty-tap.

Now Ben's a lazy
Little boy,
While Dad plays
With an exciting toy.

Mum, however,
Does the first aid.
In ways
Accidents aren't made.

I know my family's a nice little bunch
But now it's time to have my lunch.

Jessica Swift (8)
Batt CE Primary School

The Butterfly

I'm a little butterfly swirling around,
I never dream to touch the ground.

I'm a little butterfly, symmetrical that's me,
Though I can't dance like Mr Honeybee.

I'm a little butterfly swirling around,
I never dream to touch the ground.

I'm a little butterfly kissing the sky,
I smell the smell of apple pie.

I'm a little butterfly swirling around,
I never dream to touch the ground.

I'm a little butterfly looking down below,
See the children as they grow.

I'm a little butterfly swirling around,
Now finally I can touch the ground.

Ailish Butland (8)
Batt CE Primary School

The River

The river flows fast
until it reaches the sea
it hits the ship's masts
it rushes through the countryside
of the rocks it collides with,
clear blue water
fit for a king's daughter.

Hannah-Marie Black (9)
Batt CE Primary School

THE BUTTERFLY

Once I went in the garden
And I saw a marvellous thing,
It was a butterfly and
It had two painted wings.

Its antennae looked like twigs,
On top there were dots
That were really its eyes,
On the wings there were
Lots of patterns, lots and lots.

And now we come to an end
At last it had to go,
Maybe you'll see a butterfly
You will never know.

Emily Grant & Bethany Blakeley (8)
Batt CE Primary School

TREES

I hear a whistling in the breeze,
I look around at the battered leaves.
They're sitting there so sound, so still,
I watch them from the window sill.
The tree looks bare,
The tree looks weak,
I hear a sound
But very meek.
I hear them swaying in the breeze
What are those things just standing there?
Of course, they are trees.

Sian Roy (10)
Batt CE Primary School

My Secret Place

My bedroom has a secret touch
At night my toys come to life
In my room my bed starts to walk
While I'm in my secret place

My lava lamp starts to bubble
My hamster whizzes in his wheel
Have you guessed yet - where my secret place is?

I can be who I want to be
I can go wherever I wish
But listen,
'Come on now it's time for school.'

My secret place is going
It's time to leave it there
But tonight when I go back to sleep
More adventures wait for me to share.

Sophia Jackson (7)
Batt CE Primary School

Part Of My Family

My mum stays in bed, she loves it in there
My dad gets up early, he wants his cup of tea
My cousin loves football, he's football crazy
His sister is so happy she giggles all day long
And my aunty is so funny, she's mad all the time
Part of my family have got a theme but what
I have to say I'm the craziest.

Tilly Haley (8)
Batt CE Primary School

The Hullabaloo Monster

The hullabaloo monster has five eyes upon each head,
He likes to eat small children with his bread.

His body is purple, his tail is white,
He creeps around people's houses at night.

He has a monstrous body covered in yellow spots,
And on his long noses lots of green dots.

His eyes are fireballs gleaming in the sun like stars
And frightens all the people in their cars.

He causes such a stir and guess who he is . . .
He's the *hullabaloo monster!*

Christine Kemp (10)
Batt CE Primary School

Snow

I saw this white stuff fall
Today as I was out at play,
Someone said it could be snow
They could be wrong, you'll never know.

I went to bed that very night,
Waking early the sky was very bright
I looked outside and gazed with pure delight
The ground is covered and everything is white.

It was snow I saw, I'm glad to say,
We'd make a snowman this very day.

Lisa West (11)
Batt CE Primary School

LIGHTNING

Quick as a flash across the sky
Some like watching, others find it frightening
What is this, it's lightning.
Some in zigzag, some in sheet,
Appear quick as a blink
Then disappear fast as a wink.
Again and again we see it flash,
A mass of power that fills the sky
Poor unlucky people sometimes die.
All this power that comes from above
Its strength it doesn't have to prove!

Chloe Blackwell (10)
Batt CE Primary School

THE CHILD LOVERS

Central heating
Lots of food
A very good home
But still no exercise
Toys
Bed
But still no exercise
Until one day
You run abroad
Today they'll cry for you
Tomorrow they'll buy tickets.

Luke Hatton (9)
Batt CE Primary School

SUPERMARKET RAP

We boogie down the aisle
Past the apples and the peas
We're marching with the mops
And buying what we please.
We're jiving with the jellies
We're jumping with the beans
We're spinning through spaghetti
We're grooving through the greens
We're going to the checkout
We're paying at the till
We've loaded up our bags
Wow! Look at that big bill!

Amy Lockwood (10)
Batt CE Primary School

CHRISTMAS

Christmas time is full of joy,
For every little girl and boy.
The stars in the sky brightly glow,
The ground is covered in cold, wet snow.
Santa comes with his heavy sack,
Full of toys on his back.
Brings a smile to every child,
With all their new toys neatly piled.
Until next year we say goodbye,
We hoped you liked your Christmas pie.

Jodi Bradley (10)
Batt CE Primary School

Night Approaches

The end of another day slowly approaches
as the daylight softly fades into a dusky deep blue sky.

The streets are quiet and all the houses
have their curtains drawn.

The only sound is the stream at the end of the garden
with the shallow water gently trickling over the pebbles.

Stars are appearing in the sky one by one
like tiny flecks of glitter sprinkled over a soft, black velvet scarf.

The people in the houses snuggle around
the cosy warm fire.

At last it is time for them to go upstairs and have a bath
then snuggle down into their cosy warm beds and dream.

Scarlett Spalding (11)
Batt CE Primary School

In The Bath

Sitting in the bath millions of bubble mountains all around me
Swimming with my rubber duck in my little sea
With a scrub-a-dub-dub, I make myself clean
The bubble bath is my bubble machine.

I'm saturated from the hot and foamy water
I think I should get out, I know I oughta
My fingers are all shrinky, wrinkly and old
My bathtime is over, my story told.

Hannah Cook (11)
Batt CE Primary School

The Silver Horse

Galloping swiftly in the forest while it's snowing.
Jumping lively in the river while it's flowing.
Trotting happily in the field on a sunny day.
Playing with my friends on a sandy bay.
That's how I like to spend my time.
That's how I'd like to end this rhyme!

Grace Lockwood (8)
Batt CE Primary School

In The Playground

When I go in the playground
I hear lots of noise.
I block my ears so I can't hear anymore.
At five to eleven the whistle blows and we stand still.
When the whistles blows again we go to our line.
I stand like a peg, that's true and sometimes I stand like a pip!

Rebecca Dixon (9)
Berinsfield CP School

Joy

Joy is a wonderful thing to me.
Joy is just meant to be.
You can have joy when you play a game.
Even when you're with a lion that's tame.
You can have joy here and there,
You can have joy everywhere.

Lauren Hawkins (8)
Berinsfield CP School

THE SHADOWS

On a hill not far away,
Lives a cottage in its old days.
Nobody goes there, why I don't know,
Not even if they put on a show.
A man came to it that night,
He sat on a stone and had a big fright;
He saw a shadow come out of the door,
And saw lots more come out of the wall.
He started to run as fast as he could,
To get away from that horrible house.

Luke Andrews (10)
Berinsfield CP School

UNDER THE SEA

One day a shark went by a rock
Under the rock was a sock
A magic sock actually
'I will try to pull it up,' the shark said
He pulled and pulled, but he couldn't move it
The shark gave up and wished
He'd never seen the sock
And it magically disappeared . . .

Danielle Chewings (9)
Berinsfield CP School

SEASONS

The air is fresh and the fields are green
So in this case it must be spring.

The air is hot, the sky is blue
It must be summer.

The trees are brown and the leaves are falling
The season that does this is autumn.

The ground is white and the air is cold
And winter makes it freezing.

Danniel Smith (10)
Berinsfield CP School

Pets

Pets!
Lovely cuddly cat,
A hamster,
A dog whose friend was a frog.

All are different sizes
And some with lice.
Would you like a cat, be sure,
You might have less mice than before!

Leona Sweetland (9)
Berinsfield CP School

The House

But there the house lay waiting for him to return,
The phantoms listen inside ever more.
The silence outside settled on the forest's ferny floor,
The house still lay on the forest's shore.
The trees swayed as the wind blew and the shadows moved side to side,
And the owls fled as the moon laid down once again.
The sun was out and the birds were singing,
But once more the house stood in pain.
As he who knows, was drifting away into the distance.

Ricky Doran (10)
Berinsfield CP School

TEACHERS

T eachers are the best
E specially Miss Cattrall
A teacher like her
C ould never fail
H er face is so beautiful
E ven though she shouts a bit
R escue her from evil
S he is the best and she will never be sacked.

Claire Chewings (9)
Berinsfield CP School

SOUNDS AT HOME

Avon lady at the door, *ring ring*
My little brother on the floor, *bang bang*
My dad on the chair, *yawn yawn*
My big brother getting his hair, *squish squish*
My mum's cooking and frying, *sizzle sizzle*
My sister pretending to be crying, *waahh waahh.*

Amy Andrews (9)
Berinsfield CP School

TEACHERS

Teachers shout
Teachers laugh
Teachers get angry when we play up
Teachers get to sleep in the afternoon
They go to sleep about eight o'clock so they
Are ready for us the next day
In case we are naughty!

Jade Masterson (9)
Berinsfield CP School

PLAYING

P laying with friends and family
L oving and caring for each other
A nd having a good time
Y o-yos bouncing up and down
I love the sound of *boing, boing, boing*
N ext time I go out I'll give my friends a shout
G ood games to play, I play a lot every day.

Zoe Goldsbury (8)
Berinsfield CP School

RESPECT

I show respect for my mum by cooking.
I show respect for my dad by helping him.
I show respect for my sister by sharing.
I show respect for my brother by being kind.
I show respect for my little sister by caring.
I show respect for my fish by feeding them.
I show respect for myself by looking after myself.

Jessica Clarke (11)
Berinsfield CP School

A FAMILY RESPECT POEM

I show respect to my mum by doing what she says.
I show respect to my pet by looking after it.
I show respect to my brother by being nice to him.
I show respect to my dad by loving him.
I show respect to my grandma by behaving when I'm near her.
I show respect to myself by looking smart.

Darrell Pyatt (10)
Berinsfield CP School

THE TRAVELLER

The traveller rode away,
His horse left hoofprints,
He rode away very quickly,
He was riding his horse with a lot of crashes.
'I am very glad I rode away,' said the traveller,
'I like riding through the woods.'
As the horse stepped on the floor there was a creak,
The traveller stopped.
He turned around and looked into the shadows,
It was just a bit of wood.
The traveller carried on riding,
The house was watching him,
The phantom listeners were still listening to his horse riding away.
The traveller thought that he had left the house behind him,
But it just watched him in the darkness.
The traveller, still wondering why nobody was at the house, stopped
He turned around and looked.

Joanne Bumpass (10)
Berinsfield CP School

THERE'S A SHELL ON A ROCK

One day there was a shell upon a rock
And underneath there was a sock
There was another rock and
Underneath was the other sock

Whose are the socks under the rocks?
Well the person who found the shells was
Oh bother!
It's my naughty little brother.

Ben Alexander (8)
Berinsfield CP School

WINTER NIGHTS

Glittering snowflakes began to fall,
Answering the winter's call.
Not a whisper or a sound,
Came wandering from underground.

No more leaves on the trees,
No more summer breeze.
The frost piled high,
In the darkness of the winter sky.

There are no animals left here
For in winter they disappear.
The moon has gone behind the house,
Now as small as a mouse.

Who knows what will come tomorrow,
Will it be joy or sorrow?
Will this cottage stand still?
Right upon the tall green hill.

Nicola Chewings (10)
Berinsfield CP School

PLAY TIME

P lay time is a time for games
L ike tig and hide-and-seek
A nnoying teachers
Y ell sometimes

T ime and time again they shout
I t's not fair, you yell at them,
M y teacher isn't that horrid,
E ven when she's angry!

Sarah Hill (8)
Berinsfield CP School

Respect

I show respect for the teachers by doing as they say.
I show respect for my school friends by being nice to them.
I show respect for the classroom by tidying up my rubbish.
I show respect for the cooks by being polite to them.
I show respect to myself by trying to look nice.

Kimberley Greenaway (11)
Berinsfield CP School

The Cottage

The cottage stands on its own
People listened to every sound
The wind whistles
Nobody goes there, nobody will
The cottage cries in pain
It stands still
Cobwebs everywhere
The moonlight shines on every window.

Megan MacIntyre (11)
Berinsfield CP School

A Respect Poem

I respect my mum and dad by not getting in trouble.
I respect my head teacher by being sensible.
I respect my brother by letting him play with me.
I respect myself by not being silly all the time.

Daniel Selwood (10)
Berinsfield CP School

My Goal

I stand and sweat
I stare at the net
Will he go left
Or will he go right?
I kick the ball
With all my might.

He takes a dive
I kick it wide
He falls to the floor
I hear a roar
It's my best ever yet
As the ball hits the net.

The whistle blows
Full time's here
One nil to us
Get the beer!

Craig Mace (11)
Berinsfield CP School

I Wished Upon . . .

I wished upon a star
That you would love me
Thank you for making that dream come true
I wished upon the moon
That you would care for me as I care for you
Thank you for making that dream come true
And I know that you are special to me always
When I think about you
I feel like I can fly all day and night.

Jennifer Mackie (10)
Berinsfield CP School

The Object

The silent night was still,
Everything was calm,
A shadow swept over the hill,
So delicately, without any harm.

Something mysterious landed on the grass,
Its eyes focused on the tree,
Something went past,
I wonder what it could be?

A shiver went down my spine
And in a painful flash,
I heard a deafening whine
With a rumble and a crash.

I looked around,
The object was in half,
I heard another pound,
Tiny pieces were scattered down the path.

Suddenly the object was not in sight
Leaving behind the bitter night.

Tallulah Allmond (10)
Berinsfield CP School

Valentine's

Valentine's is lovely
Valentine's is blue
Valentine's is my best time
Because I'm with you.

Bradley Taylor (10)
Berinsfield CP School

The Traveller

The traveller rode off into the distance,
Leaving slushy hoofprints behind,
The house was watching and waiting all alone in the darkness.
Everything was still and quiet,
Noting to be seen or nothing to be heard,
But still looking into the distance,
The moonlight was shining all over the forest's floor,
Leaving the shadows all alone and undisturbed.
The trees were rustling
And waiting for the traveller to come back,
But nothing happened.
The slushy hoofprints started to disappear.
The house was still,
Watching and waiting,
But the traveller rode off
In the distant darkness, all alone.

Lucy Scotland
Berinsfield CP School

Respect

I show respect for the teachers by not speaking when they are teaching.
I show respect to my friends by letting them play with me.
I show respect to the head teacher by being polite.
I show respect to my work by keeping it neat.
I show respect to the classroom by keeping it tidy.
I show respect throughout the school by being kind.
I show respect to everyone by helping them in the playground
And everywhere around school.

Simean Cullen (10)
Berinsfield CP School

A Respected Poem

I show respect for my mum by
Tidying my room and helping her out.

I show respect for my dad by
Doing what I have been told.

I show respect for my brother by
Being kind and considerate to him.

I show respect for my sister by
Looking out for her.

I show respect for my sister by
Looking after her and playing with her.

I show respect for my cousins by
Being there all the time.

I show respect to my aunties by
Doing what I have been told.

Gary Jones (11)
Berinsfield CP School

My Name

My name is Fred, I've got a big head.
When I go to school I act the fool.
So maybe I should stay at home in bed each day,
But my mum said if I stay at home in bed
I won't be very bright, cos I won't learn to read and write,
So I think that I should go to school with little Joe!

Fred Mummery (11)
Berinsfield CP School

SUMMER GARDEN

Growing blooming all around,
The sun shimmering in the sky,
Fields of blossom and flowers
Oak tree growing tall and high
Nothing too glum, nothing to frown
Just things you love are all around.

In the sky, no cloud can be seen,
Just a blue sky, bright and sweet,
Seeing this will make you happy,
In here there's nothing but heat.

Down below on the ground
You can see groups of flowers.
Everything so beautiful,
You could stay in here for hours.

Jessica Matthews (11)
Berinsfield CP School

THE TRAVELLER

The traveller rode off trying desperately not to look back,
The horse trying not to slip,
The house stood alone in the dark,
Watching and waiting for the traveller to come back.
The trees swaying gently in the wind,
The cold made him gasp and clutch the reins,
The road ahead shone in the moonlight,
When the sound of the clanging hooves were gone,
The traveller would never come back.

Chloe Somerville (11)
Berinsfield CP School

THE FEARS OF WINTER

In the frosty morning,
When dusk appears,
The wind tells us
Of nameless fears.

The world will end
In a few months or so
And we won't hear happiness
And we wont' hear woe.

There will be nothing,
Nothing to do
And we won't get anything,
Nothing new.

Phillip McFarland (11)
Berinsfield CP School

ANIMALS

Animals are bright and some are helpful to others.
Some are cruel and can bite and scratch.
Some are bumpy and some are smooth,
Some play with people, while some are colourful
And change colour and play tricks.

Some eat flowers, some drink flowers,
Bears like fish or salmon, baboons have colourful faces,
Cats live in the street, some animals like people,
Pigs like mud and make a noise.

Loyde Harwood (10)
Berinsfield CP School

War Poem

People, people here and there,
Rushing about everywhere,
Lots of people scared stiff,
The smell of the bomb is a bad whiff.
Soldiers moving with their guns,
While mothers run away with their sons.
As big crowds start shouting,
The people move while the bombs are melting.
People go and collect their masks,
While others go and get lots of flasks.
People rushing round at last,
While things go silent very fast.

Katie Marshall (11)
Berinsfield CP School

Tommy

Tommy is my little cat
He likes to curl up on the mat
In front of the fire he likes to sit
He will lay there for quite a bit
Until his dinner he will lay
Before he goes out to play

As soon as he hears the yellow school bus
He will run back in to have some fuss
He really is a lazy cat
Wouldn't it be nice to be like that!

Amy Light (10)
Berinsfield CP School

The Cottage

In the mist of the midnight sky
  stood the creepiest cottage.
It was as black as deep desires
  And as black as the midnight sky.
The stairs were as crooked as crooked nails
  And as squeaky as a mouse
And as weak as a newborn baby
  And just as strong as thin wood.
The rooms were weird and shocking
  Because of all the creepy webs.

Nico Honer (11)
Berinsfield CP School

Nobody's More Annoying Than My Sister!

My sister is a devil.
Her target's to be annoying.
She does it every day.
In every single way.
Her second name is 'destroy'.
It's a good way to describe her.
But I could think of worse like 'kick'
And 'punch' and 'stir'.
The words 'good' and 'nice' and 'fair'
Do not apply to her, as she likes
Making people rip out their hair!
Most people wonder why I'm not like her
It must be because I'm a little star.

Danielle Mullett (9)
Brize Norton Primary School

WHO NEEDS A SISTER?

Who needs a sister?
Who needs a sister?
All they do is nark at you
And sometimes even bark at you.

Who needs a sister?
Who needs a sister?
Because all they do is argue with you
And sometimes ignore you too.

Who needs a sister?
Who needs a sister?
I need a sister because she's always there for me,
I need a sister because she will always care for me.

Bethany Forty (10)
Brize Norton Primary School

WHO NEEDS A COUSIN?

Who needs a cousin to wash your face?
Who needs a cousin to do up your lace?
Who needs a cousin to cry on their shoulder?
Who needs a cousin to say, 'Behave, you're getting older!'
Who needs a cousin to help you with your homework?
Who needs a cousin to dish out the dessert?
Who needs a cousin to brush your hair?
Who needs a cousin to love and to care?
Who needs a cousin to call out your name?
I can't perceive a life without cousins,
Nothing would be the same!

Jessica Harper (11)
Brize Norton Primary School

WHO NEEDS MONSTERS?

Demons howling,
Beavers growling,
Who needs monsters? I don't.
Monsters, monsters everywhere.

Bears bothering
Wolves hovering
Who needs monsters? I don't.
Monsters, monsters everywhere.

Ghosts haunting
Ghosts flaunting
Who needs monsters? I don't.
Monsters, monsters everywhere.

Sh, sh, don't say a word.
No doubt about it
Hide, hide away
Darkness everywhere!

Who needs monsters?

Alicia McCrudden (11)
Brize Norton Primary School

FRIENDS

Friends are fun,
They share their feelings and friendship.
Friends are kind,
They don't do nasty things,
They don't fight either,
The whole world should be friends!

Sarah Bellenger (9)
Brize Norton Primary School

WHO NEEDS A BROTHER?

Who needs a brother?
Who needs a brother?
All they do is argue
But if you are lucky, you can too
Who needs a brother?
Who needs a brother?

Who needs a brother?
Who needs a brother?
All they do is scare you
And even when you are on the loo!
Who needs a brother?
Who needs a brother?

I need a brother!
I need a brother!
To care for me
And to help me on things that I do not know.
I need a brother!
I need a brother!

Sophie Howard (11)
Brize Norton Primary School

BEWARE

Beware of my rabbit that scratches and kicks.
Beware of my brother who punches and flicks.
Beware of my dad who roars like thunder.
Beware of my mum who screams with a plunder.
Beware of my sister who is always being lazy,
But most of all beware of *me!*

Stephanie Lett (9)
Brize Norton Primary School

HUMPY DUMPTY

Humpty Dumpty sat on a chair
Humpty Dumpty flew up in the air
Little young Larry chuckled with glee,
'Just what I wanted, omelette for tea.'
Little Larry laughed a lot
My my my what a plot
So Larry went to sleep day and night
Then Humpty Dumpty started a fight
Little Larry got a punch
Then Humpty Dumpty got a crunch
Then Larry cracked Humpty Dumpty's head
Then Larry went to bed.
Did Larry know Humpty Dumpty was asleep?
Maybe Larry had a peep.

Richard Oxlade (9)
Brize Norton Primary School

A HEART OF STEEL

She's never given up, she's always been so nice,
But why did she have to go?
I don't know, do you?

She's helped me through my heartbreaks,
She's helped me through everything,
She truly did have a heart of steel.

She's never gone wrong, she's always been right,
Now that's a fact!

She's always been a friend,
She'll be here forever.

Liam Masson (10)
Brize Norton Primary School

That Silly Old Cat

There was an old crooked cat
Who always sat on the mat
The mat caught fire
The cat jumped higher
And that was the end of that!

Adam Lee Williams (11)
Brize Norton Primary School

A Load Of Nonsense

Down by the orange trees and red tufty tuffs,
You will see some rhino righty flower fluff.
It will grow and grow and grow some more,
Until it reaches ten foot four.

It grew about ten foot tall and three metres wide,
The jungle shook when he stepped inside!

Ben File (10)
Brize Norton Primary School

My Mum

My mum is cool, even though she can shout very loudly,
My mum is the best mum in the world to me.
My mum is thoughtful and kind,
My mum's name is Sharron and it's very cool to me.

Charlotte Taylor (10)
Brize Norton Primary School

The Old Man From Hull

There was an old man from Hull
Who liked to look at seagulls
He went to the seaside
And got washed away in a tide
That poor old man from Hull!

Hannah Phillipson (11)
Brize Norton Primary School

A Limerick

There was a lady from China
Whose husband was a miner
There was a big *boom*
And he ended up in a tomb
That poor lady from China.

Samuel Bayliss (11)
Brize Norton Primary School

The Gazelle From Belfast

There was a gazelle from Belfast
Who tried to drive fast
He went to the vet
And lost on a bet
The foolish gazelle from Belfast.

Kyle Bishop (11)
Brize Norton Primary School

Poetry

Poetry can be funny,
Poetry can be strange,
But the one thing I like most;
Is poetry that makes no sense at all.

Poetry can be weird,
Poetry can be odd,
But the one thing I like most;
Is poetry that makes no sense at all.

Poetry can be obscure,
Poetry can be amazing,
But the one thing I like most;
Is poetry that makes no sense at all.

Poetry is my favourite form of writing
And that's the way I want it to stay!

Toby Stanton (10)
Brize Norton Primary School

Nowhere

N owhere is a simple place,
O n a distant moon.
W here little Joo-Jub people live,
H earing every word we say.
E verybody tries to fly there,
R ockets, planes and all,
E veryone always fails and then begins to fall.

Andrew Porter (11)
Carswell Primary School

My Baby Brother

My baby brother
is cute and cuddly
with one string of hair.

He cries a lot
doesn't stop
all night long.

If you give him some food
he dribbles it out all over
his clean Babygro.

But I love him
all the same
as anything else
in the world.

Lois Amber Jamieson (8)
Carswell Primary School

Winter

Winter's cool and frosty,
A time when people are frozen.
For the animals it's hibernating time,
Everybody's inside.
The ground is covered with snow
And footprints stay where they went.
I look out of the window and see a car on tow,
I hope spring comes soon.
The only thing I would say that is good
Is the beautiful sight of the moon.

Jacob Walcott (10)
Carswell Primary School

My Teacher Is . . .

M arvellous
Y oung

T errifying (sometimes)
E njoys teaching (sometimes)
A nxious
C ourageous
H appy
E nthusiastic
R ipe as an apple

I llustrated
S haky (sometimes)
.
.
.

Daniel Lock (11)
Carswell Primary School

The Love

I love my dog
He's my best friend
His name is Buster

I love my family
They make me feel fuzzy inside
All of the time

I love chocolate
It is nice
It is the best of the lot!

Shane Jordan (10)
Carswell Primary School

ANIMALS

Animals, animals
Cats, sheep and cattle
Birds with their *tu-whit tu-whoos*
Dogs with toys that rattle.

Animals, animals
Have homes in the trees
Like birds and insects
And chimpanzees.

Animals, animals
I have a tortoise called Todd
I think he's lovely
You may think he's odd.

Animals, animals
Dolphins are so sweet
Whales and penguins
All kinds of fish they eat.

Sophie Sillman (8)
Carswell Primary School

MY TEACHER IS . ..

T rustworthy
E nraged
A ctive
C areful
H armless (hopefully!)
E xtraordinary
R espectful.

Michelle-Rose Sherwood (9)
Carswell Primary School

My School

I like my teacher
She's really nice
I just hope
She doesn't have headlice.

I think school
Is really cool
I just wish
It had a swimming pool.

I think maths
Is really great
I can already
Count up to eight.

I like writing
That doesn't make me sad
But I hate homework
It drives me mad.

Lauren Elms (9)
Carswell Primary School

Cupid

Love is important it's simply the best,
My boyfriend is better than all the rest.

I believe in love in many different ways,
Spending time with you on hot summer days.

So on Valentine's Day I love you with all my heart,
So we will never be apart.

Louise Mortimer (11)
Carswell Primary School

I Like My PlayStation

I like my PlayStation

L ucky PlayStation
I t is quite small
K racing games
E very day I play with it

M any games
Y ou wait when it loads

P laying all day
L ooking for a game to play
A lways playing it
Y ou like the games
S taring when I am playing it
T ekron
A PlayStation has good graphics
T omb Raider
I t is good
O nly one
N umber one!

Henry Thomas (10)
Carswell Primary School

My Baby Sister

My baby sister is like a soft, cuddly teddy bear,
She is always smiling and laughing,
But not until she screams the house down.
She gets in a mood,
But eventually falls asleep,
I like my baby sister but only when she is calm!

Hannah Greenaway (9)
Carswell Primary School

In The Spooky House

Into the spooky house
Into the spooky house
You will find a murdered body
Next to a creepy mouse.

Down in the sewer lane
Down in the sewer lane
You will find toxic waste
That will give you lots of pain.

In the dirty dam
In the dirty dam
When you cook
There's something that swam.

In the broken ballroom
In the broken ballroom
There's a party going on
But the disco goes *boom!*

Macaully Spraggs (9)
Carswell Primary School

I Love You

I love you because I do.
When I see you I go crazy
Because I adore you.

When I see you I go tingly inside.
On Friday it is Valentine's,
I am Romeo and you can be
My Juliet.

Sean Farrell (11)
Carswell Primary School

My Favourite Animal

Animals, animals
I like them all,
even though they
are big and small.

Cats are nice,
dogs are best,
better than
all the rest.

Animals, animals
tall and tiny,
whales and dolphins
nice and shiny.

Hamsters are sweet
but guinea pigs are cuter,
even more fun than
my computer.

Lily Cooper (8)
Carswell Primary School

Love Poem

L ove is all around us,
O ur body needs lots of love,
V alentine's is when love is about,
E veryone loves someone.

P eople don't like love,
O ne of them is me,
E veryone loves their mum,
M aybe their dad too.

Craig Connolly (9)
Carswell Primary School

My Cute Hamster

My hamster is tiny
Smaller than a mouse
Has a little cage
But calls it his house.

My hamster has a ball
But he doesn't use it at all
He only uses his ball
When he is feeling cool.

My hamster pretends
He is at school
But he always
Takes his ball.

I love my hamster
He's cuddly and kind
The only thing is
He snores in the night!

Ellie Adams (9)
Carswell Primary School

Love For My Niece

My baby niece, Ella,
She has long, curly, orange hair.

She calls James, 'James,'
And she calls Grandma, 'Grandma,'
And she calls Mummy, 'Mummy.'
She's the best niece that can be.
She can be a bad-tempered madam,
But she's the best niece that can be.

James Irving (9)
Carswell Primary School

I Love

I love Monday
because it is a noisy day
I love Tuesday
because it is a lazy day
I love Wednesday
because it is a good day to play
I love Thursday
because it is a quiet day
I love Friday
because I can do everything my own way
I love Saturday
because it is an excellent day
I love Sunday
because it is a roast dinner day.

Jack Meacey (9)
Carswell Primary School

I've Seen

I've seen a lion roar in the sun,
I've seen a robin run.
I've seen a jaguar chase a rabbit,
I've seen a zebra's very bad habit.
I've seen a monkey and a hare,
I've seen the feathers of a grizzly bear.
I've seen an ill snake laugh and play,
I've seen the rain of a sunny day.
I've seen the lies that nature does tell,
I've seen the jungle when it's well.
But what I haven't seen is this,
A poem that ends with a kiss!

Elisha Fiddaman (10)
Carswell Primary School

Cupid

Cupid, Cupid are you there?
Cupid, in your underwear
Cupid, Cupid are you here?
Cupid, Cupid are you near?

Cupid, Cupid where are you
Are you with your *luuurve* crew?
Cupid, Cupid is that you?
Cupid in my trainer shoe.

Cupid, Cupid come at once!
Cupid you are not a dunce!
Aim your arrow at that girl,
She really makes my head twirl.

Cupid, Cupid are you there?
Cupid, in your underwear.
Cupid, Cupid are you near?
Cupid, Cupid are you here?

Harry Rennells McCarthy (9)
Carswell Primary School

Love

My first girlfriend was Tollie,
We played together.
We played on her Nintendo,
We played Super Mario 3.
We hugged each other,
She gave me a picture of her.
I really love her and we will
See each other again.

Robert Webster (11)
Carswell Primary School

FOOTBALL

Football is cool
I play it outside
Till time to go
Football is the best
Better than the rest.

Football is fun
I love playing it outside
Till time to go
Football is wicked
The ball you have to kick it.

Football is great
I play it outside
I play till it's time to go
Football is sound
You curl the ball around.

Dale Paterson (11)
Carswell Primary School

WHAT IS LOVE?

Love is sweet.
With the skylight stars it shines on you
When you say the word, love is romantic.
It will help you on your way.
Love is bright, it's waiting for you as you walk your way.
Love is a fortune in your life.
Without it what would you do?
Love is here in your life, everywhere around you.
You cannot see it but you know it's in the world somewhere.
What is love? Does anybody know?

Meagan Littlejohns (10)
Carswell Primary School

Cute Boys

Out of all the boys I've ever seen
In my life,
The cutest one
I truly can't describe.

He's not like any other boy,
He doesn't like football,
He doesn't like football toys,
He is kind of tall.

He does not know I like him,
Him, I always miss,
Should I ever tell him?
His name is . . .

Rachel Hayden (10)
Carswell Primary School

My Mum

My mum is great,
She is never late,
My mum is the best,
She won't rest,
Until we're happy,
She's been doing that since we've been in nappies.
My mum smells like roses
And she can massage your toesies.
My mum likes fashion
And she gives us our ration.
My mum makes me laugh,
As she leads us down the rickety path.
That's my mum and she's a whole lot more.

Lauren Gill (9)
Carswell Primary School

Love Poem

L ove is not for me
O nly girls like it
V ery sickly
E veryone's gone mad!

Steven Dann (9)
Carswell Primary School

I Love My . . .

I love my PlayStation,
I love my games,
I love all of my paper aeroplanes.
My Gameboy's great,
I love the school fête,
I love all my food,
I love it when my brothers are rude.
I love to fight with my brothers,
I love to fall asleep under the covers,
But the best thing I love and like
Is my shiny, beautiful bike.

Mason Kelley (9)
Carswell Primary School

Love Is Not For Me

L ove is not for me, it's not my cup of tea,
O yeah, when I see someone kiss I go, 'Oh gee.'
V alentine's is sickly and soppy,
E very time I get a Valentine's card I get stroppy!

Ryan Cleary (10)
Carswell Primary School

PEACE

Peace is white,
It smells like flowers in the spring.
Peace tastes like candyfloss,
It sounds like waves lapping at the shore.
Peace lives in the heart of you.

Cameron Lumsden (10)
Carswell Primary School

MAKING A MONSTER POTION

Take a hand like a dragon
A body as red as blood
And teeth as pointed as needles.
Add some scary eyes to your potion
And some teeth as green as you!
Then add a hound's body to your potion
Then you have made a dragon potion.

Watch your step!

Anna-Lee Evans (8)
Carswell Primary School

PEACE

Peace is white,
It smells like flowers in spring.
Peace tastes like candyfloss,
It sounds like waves lashing at the shore.
Peace feels soft and fluffy,
Peace lives inside your heart.

Jamie-Lee Burgoyne (9)
Carswell Primary School

SEASONS

S pecial
P ansies
R ain
I ce
N ewborn lambs
G reat baby chicks

S unny
U nikely to snow
M essy
M elting ice cream
E ating junk food
R ed, bright sun

A pple picking
U mbrellas
T rees being cut down
U nder trees leaves, acorns fall
M ice
N escafé, hot chocolate

W indy/snowy
I cy igloos
N oisy: singing, dancing
T rees for Christmas
E verlasting light
R udolph.

Danielle Young (11)
Carswell Primary School

FLOWERS

In the morning they start their day,
They grow and grow to suit their way.
By nightfall they're asleep in bed,
They are tired and want to rest their head.

They are pink and blue,
Red and orange too.
Black and white,
It's dark as night.

Heleena Smith (10)
Carswell Primary School

MERMAIDS

Mermaids' fins are like a fish's tail,
all their bodies are colourful,
shells and fish, nice and bright colours.
Beautiful long hair
may have a colourful home
flutter their fins in the glittering sea.
They swim with the dolphins,
play with the fish,
pop their heads out of the water
and look at the boats and the humans
on the beach.
Sometimes the mermaids are bored with the water
maybe like a princess but sick of the sea,
maybe rich, maybe not.
Mermaids' fins may be glittery
mermaids have fun in the sea
and sing with the dolphins.
The weeds sway when they go past
the swirling bubbles wind around them.
Mermaids are beautiful
they have lots of fun.
I wish I could sing and dance and swim
with the dolphins.
I wish I was a dolphin.

Paige Taylor (8)
Carswell Primary School

POP STARS

Gareth Gates is a pop star,
Rockin', rockin', on his new guitar.
Girls Aloud, Girls Aloud,
Oh what a racket! Oh what a sound!

Good Charlotte are the best,
Rockin' and rockin' in an old vest.
Britney Spears is on the line,
Hit Me Baby One More Time.

Blue, Blue, Blue,
They've got the flu.
Will Young,
Come On Baby Light My Fire,
That's what he sang.

Shadé McGaw (10)
Carswell Primary School

MY NAME IS MEGAN

Hello my name is Megan,
My second name is Bell.
I love my dad and sister
And they love me as well.

I have a nana and grampy,
They buy me lots of things,
Like clothes and shoes and ice creams
And many other things.

I have an auntie Vicky and uncle Lee
With two of my best cousins,
Thomas and Sophie.

Megan Bell (10)
Carswell Primary School

SPRING

Spring is here
It's the best time of year
Flowers growing
The sun is glowing
Spring is finally here!

Spring is here
No snow storms to fear
Animals are coming out of hibernation
It's a huge sensation
Spring is finally here!

Spring is here
Summer is near
People going on holidays
No more rainy days
Spring is finally here!

Emma Finch (11)
Carswell Primary School

MY BEST FRIENDS

My best friends
Will be there for me.
My best friends
Will help me when I'm sad.
My best friends
Will never leave me.
My best friends
Will laugh with me.
My best friends
Will follow me forever.

Bryony Gledhill (9)
Carswell Primary School

SNOWFLAKES

Snowflakes falling on the ground,
Snowflakes fall without a sound,
Snowflakes falling from the sky,
Snowflakes getting in my eyes,
Snowflakes everywhere, all around.

Lisa Roberts (9)
Carswell Primary School

HOW TO MAKE A MONSTER

Get some teeth as sharp as daggers
And a body as black as death
And some ears as pointed as pyramids!

Get some scales as smooth as a snake
And claws as sharp as pins
And you have made a *monster!*

Be scared, be very scared!

Philip Gray (8)
Carswell Primary School

LOVE

Love is the colour of red,
Love smells like roses,
Love tastes sweet,
Love sounds romantic and peaceful,
Love feels warm and soft,
Love lives in the middle of your heart.

Leia Wilkinson (11)
Carswell Primary School

Monsters

I saw a monster under my bed
I can't get to sleep tonight
Window with curtains blowing in my face
The ceiling's cracking above my head.
By sharp, pointed teeth will the monster eat me?
I hope not because he might hurt me
And I'm scared half of my life.

Joseph Samways (8)
Carswell Primary School

Arctic

A rctic is white
R ough and tough ice is
C lover patches none are there
T all mountains you can't climb
I celand it is
C lear like a white bed sheet.

Lee McAulay (10)
Carswell Primary School

The Wizard

The wizard is small and magical and black as a shadow
His beard is like snow
And his staff is crooked and twisted
His hat points like a finger with bright, big stars on it.
The boots he wears are curled at the toe
And his cloak of velvet falls to the floor
And he's under my bed . . .

Nathan Singh (8)
Carswell Primary School

FLOWERS

When the sun comes out they start their day
And watch the children playing,
They wave in the wind and dance and play,
Whilst each little flower sings.

Different colours, shapes and sizes too,
We see them everywhere.
Oh no! The sun is going down,
But we will see them tomorrow you'll see!

Each day I come out,
My leaves I sprout,
My pollen is sweet for bees to eat,
But as days go by I start to die.

Charlotte Rawcliffe (11)
Carswell Primary School

LOVE AND CARING

L ove is so important
O love is so imaginative
V ery special to everyone
E veryone loves each other.

C an you feel it spreading?
A nice feeling to feel
R eally brilliant feeling
I love to care
N ever stop loving
G ive love to people.

Emma Thomas (9)
Carswell Primary School

My Teacher

My teacher is funny,
When she's mad she is like a furious bunny.
She is red with laughter,
Sometimes an elephant's dafter.

My teacher is clever,
She never wears leather.
She makes me read,
It's boring for me.

English is boring too,
I say boo.
Reading is cool,
Especially in school.

Max Simmonds (9)
Carswell Primary School

Best Friend

B est bud ever
E very day I see her
S he's always there for me
T he one I can trust.

F orever friends
R eally cool
I s the best
E ndless friendship
N ever horrible to me
D ifferent to all my other friends.

Codie-Leigh Soames (11)
Carswell Primary School

TIGER

T hey are cute and cuddly
I ncredible creatures
G rizzly and cool and fast animals
E at a lot of meat and other animals
R eally good to watch them.

Rhys Brandon (10)
Carswell Primary School

MY PONY, STAR

Over the hills, far away,
All day me and my pony go out to play.
Star's so soft, she glistens like a star.

Star rarely bites
And she's almost white.
Over the hills and far away,
All day me and my pony go out to play.

Emily Mullord (9)
Carswell Primary School

MY LOVE POEM

L ovely you are
O nly you in my heart
V ery nice, yes you are
E ven when you're sad.

Laura Johns (9)
Carswell Primary School

A Goal For The Fans

Premiership is cool
Barthez is a fool
Goals are scored
Then the crowd roared
Goals are saved
The final is paved
The final is won
We've had some fun
The score was close
Some of the players had an overdose.

World Cup is better
Starts with my best letter
Brazil won last time
They only eat limes
The French are the worst
Some of the players were going to burst
England did well
Some players fell
Germany came second
They did good I reckon.

None of the players bowl
Each player scores a goal
Football's great
I always play it with a mate
It's totally fun
But they don't play it in the sun
It's sometimes a draw
But it doesn't start a war
Man United are the best
Better than all the rest.

Jamie Smith (10)
Carswell Primary School

FRIENDS

Friends are nice
Friends are silly
My friend is big
And he's called Billy
He makes me laugh
And shares his scarf.
When I am lonely
He sits by me
He cheers me up
When I am sad.

Carl Fuller (8)
Carswell Primary School

THE SEA

The wavy sea goes *swish, swash*
A big, strong wave came
And the sea monster came too
He came home with me.
I was scared all of the night
I would not look under my bed
Because I heard rumbles and grumbles
All of the time.

Courtney Rutty (9)
Carswell Primary School

SUMMER

In the summer we play outside,
On climbing frames or on the slide;
We eat ice cream and have lots of fun
And we sunbathe under the sun.

We run about,
Whilst children shout;
We go on holiday far, far away,
On a warm, sunny day.

Lauren Brant (10)
Carswell Primary School

Love And Caring

L uck for everyone
O h love is so important
V ery special
E veryone can feel love.

C are for everyone
A ll you want is love
R oses are red
I maginative
N ice
G orgeous you are.

Stacey Robinson (9)
Carswell Primary School

Recipe For A Mermaid

Take a fin as green as seaweed,
Blue rocks as blue as blueberries,
A crown as green as rocks,
Teeth as white as chisels,
Eyes as blue as the sky,
Skin as white as a star.

Renee Darling (9)
Carswell Primary School

I Love My Dogs

I love my dogs

L ucky Lady
O nly one
V ery good
E very day they look at me.

M oaning dogs
Y earning every second -

D ogs like to bark
O nly once a day
G ood runners
S orry when they bite you.

Leon Farquhar (10)
Carswell Primary School

Mummies

Mummies are found
Deep in the ground
Where the Egyptians put them long ago.
They are wrapped in bandages
With lots of layers
And some of them were richer
Than football players.

They are skeletons now and in museums
And some of their heads have come off
And they smell of horrible stuff.

Amy Finch (11)
Carswell Primary School

THERE WAS A WITCH

The witch has a face as green as grass,
A cape as black as the night sky,
A long nose like a sharp pencil,
A brown broomstick like the bark of a tree
And shoes as clumpy as horses' hooves.
The witch has a lovely cat called Chats
That loves to eat bats
And a duck that lives in the bath
That always goes *quack, quack.*
Her hair is blue
And she sings her favourite tune!

Katie Bell (8)
Carswell Primary School

DOLPHINS

Dolphins are blue
They live in the sea
They curl and twirl
Then sing for me
Their voice sounds like a bumblebee
So soft and sweet
And just for me
They swim so slowly
Making waves
As they swim so carefully and gently
Like a lullaby.

Ashleigh Brant (8)
Carswell Primary School

THE MONSTER

The monster
looks like
an ugly spot
the size of a ten foot pot.

He eats
people in a
baby sock
with chickenpox.

He has a
pet-eating clock
and very big socks
with lots of warthogs.

Never be scared
of a *monster!*

Monsters
are not real!

Monsters
are your imagination!

The monster
looks like
an ugly spot
the size of a ten foot pot.

Monsters are
just stuff
that you picture in your head.

Carl Powell (9)
Carswell Primary School

I Am The Captain Of My Ship

I am the captain of my ship,
I like to sail the coast near Bristol
And if anyone gets in my way,
I'll shoot them with my pistol.

I am the captain of my ship
And a bloodthirsty pirate am I,
For if I'm ever annoyed at all,
I'll stab you in the eye!

I am the captain of my ship,
I love to shoot my gun,
My goal would be to rule the world,
My hobby's bossing everyone.

I am the captain of my ship,
I have a million stupid slaves,
Each dumb, ugly and gross,
Their voices sound like wooden claves.

I am the captain of my ship,
I find myself quite cool,
I like to boogie all night long
And that will be all.

I am the captain of my ship
And I am captain alone,
With my ship I'll have to sink,
Just save my mobile phone!

Alice Samways (9)
Carswell Primary School

On The Night I Was Born

On the night I was born, the earth shook.
On the night I was born, the angels sang.
On the night I was born, the stars danced with delight.
On the night I was born, they gave me a cute teddy bear.
On the night I was born, my grandparents came to greet me.
On the night I was born, they gave me a blanket made of gold silk.
On the night I was born, the church bells rang.
On the night I was born, they said I was lovely.

Megan Robertson (11)
Chalgrove Community Primary School

On My 11th Birthday

On my 11th birthday my dad cheered and jumped around,
On my 11th birthday I got some very pretty fish,
On my 11th birthday I had enough money to go to Uranus,
On my 11th birthday the stars were shining brightly,
On my 11th birthday my nan cried a river,
On my 11th birthday I got crowned a king,
On my 11th birthday I became even more special,
On my 11th birthday I was 11, just 11.

Sean Ayres (11)
Chalgrove Community Primary School

On The Day My Cat Died

On the day my cat died, I cried all night.
On the day my cat died, it was a shock.
On the day my cat died, it was a fright.
On the day my cat died, I was afraid.

On the day my cat died, it was very sad.
On the day my cat died, I wanted to die.
On the day my cat died, I was speechless,
At least he's in peace.

Tom Bruce (10)
Chalgrove Community Primary School

On The Night I Was Born

On the night I was born, my life had just begun.
On the night I was born, my dad held me for the first time.
On the night I was born, my brother came to greet me.
On the night I was born, my gran sang to me.
On the night I was born, they gave me a blanket made of purple silk.
On the night I was born, the sky turned red.
On the night I was born, my dad made me a cot out of wood.
On the night I was born, I felt all special inside.

Rosie Ling (11)
Chalgrove Community Primary School

On My First Birthday

On my first birthday, I woke in my cot.
On my first birthday, my mum carried me down
And there were lots of guests.
On my first birthday, I had all my friends with me
And everybody was smiling at me.
On my first birthday, I was so happy with my presents.
My first birthday I will never forget.

Robert Coles (11)
Chalgrove Community Primary School

The Day I Got My Cat

The day I got my cat, it was magic and all my dreams came true.
The day I got my cat, I couldn't believe my eyes.
The day I got my cat, I was crying with joy.
The day I got my cat, she had fur like a cloud,
Her whiskers were like propellers and her eyes like balloons.
The day I got my cat, it was the best day of my life.

Sean Jackson (11)
Chalgrove Community Primary School

The Day I Went On Holiday

The day I went on holiday, the beautiful sun rose.
The day I went on holiday, the deep blue sea was magical.
The day I went on holiday, I felt the soft sand under my feet.
The day I went on holiday, the bright sky made me feel
Like I never wanted to leave.
The day I left my holiday, it was too short.

Mattie Walton (10)
Chalgrove Community Primary School

The Day I Was Born

The day that I was born, my mum started crying.
When I was born, my nan squeezed me so much.
When I was born, everyone got the champagne out
Because I was wonderful.
When I was born, everyone loved me and cuddled me
And it looked like people were lining up to give me a cuddle.

Lindsay Turner (11)
Chalgrove Community Primary School

THE DAY I . . .

The day I learnt to read, England won the World Cup.
The day I leant to swim, I went to the beach in Spain.
The day I learnt to walk, it felt like I was walking in space.
The day I learnt to kick, I scored 3 past Oli Kahn.
The day I learnt to talk, the words kept spilling out.
The day I was born was the best day of my life.

Daniel Lamb (10)
Chalgrove Community Primary School

WHEN I WAS BORN

When I was born my mum said I was wonderful.
When I was born my mum cuddled me.
When I was born my dad felt happy and everyone was smiling.
When I was born the church bells rang.

Anthony Collins (10)
Chalgrove Community Primary School

WHEN I HAD MY BIRTHDAY

When I had my birthday, my mum gave me her love.
When I had my birthday, my dad gave me his heart.
When I had my birthday, my sister gave me her blood.
When I had my birthday, my family gave me their souls,
And when I said thank you, I wished them
Hope, joy, love, happiness and safety.

Jake Rudman (10)
Chalgrove Community Primary School

Five Senses

On the day I was born I felt my grandad's soul,
On the day I was born I felt my family's spirit,
On the day I was born I tasted the universe,
On the day I was born I tasted the air of God,
On the day I was born I saw the stars in the sky,
On the day I was born I saw my parents greeting me,
On the day I was born I smelt the elements around me,
On the day I was born I smelt the summer rain,
On the day I was born I heard the angels around me,
On the day I was born I heard my destiny starting,
On the day I was born I came down from Heaven again.

Samuel Peris (10)
Chalgrove Community Primary School

On The Night Before Christmas

On the night before Christmas, I laid in my bed.
On the night before Christmas, I heard rustling.
On the night before Christmas, I tiptoed downstairs.
On the night before Christmas, the clock struck twelve.
On the night before Christmas, I heard some bells and saw a shadow on the roof.
All this led to one thing, I was sure it was Santa, but
It was my hamster's shadow!

Michaela Wiltshire (10)
Chalgrove Community Primary School

On My First Birthday

On my first birthday I sat and thought, *what a special boy I am.*
I looked around at everybody who was wishing me a happy birthday.

I looked around at all the people and thought,
are those big presents for me or somebody else?
It brought tears to my eyes,
everybody was laughing and joking just for me.
It was night, I looked up at the bright yellow stars,
circling around me, a full, bright moon reflecting into the pond.
How lovely it looked with the fish swimming in the pond.

How special I am.

Craig Wyatt (10)
Chalgrove Community Primary School

The Day I Was Born

On the day I was born, I thought I saw the universe spinning.
On the day I was born, I though I saw the stars singing.
On the day I was born, I thought I saw the sky dancing.
On the day I was born, I thought I saw my mum crying.
On the day I was born, I thought I saw my mum cuddling me.
On the day I was born, I thought I saw my dad crying.
On the day I was born, I thought I saw my dad dancing.
On the day I was born, I thought I saw my mum crack open a bottle.
On the day I was born, I thought I saw the sun shining.

Alysha Dix (10)
Chalgrove Community Primary School

KENNING DOG

Cat-chaser,
Good-racer,
Fierce-fighter,
Soft-biter,
Puppy-eyes,
Big-sighs,
Wall-jumper,
My-lumper,
Biscuit-binner,
Huge-sinner,
Lap-sitter,
Disco-hitter,
Best-friend,
Toy-lender . . .

Jessica Marsh (10)
Dr South's CE Primary School

FLOODS

Rain falls day after day,
Water slowly rising,
People panicking as they get closed in,
Men lift their children onto rooftops,
Parents scrambling to the highest level,
Homeless get washed away as they have nowhere to go,
Loads of food goes to waste,
Tears fall as houses get demolished,
Crops drown in the water.
People are relieved as the flood dies down,
Years of work are needed to catch up on their lives.

William Brown (11)
Dr South's CE Primary School

Morgan le Fay

(From the story of King Arthur)

Morgan le Fay was a woman with long, black hair.
She wore a gown made from animal skins,
Which she looked after with great care.
She had great taste and skill for magic,
With which she made a tale so tragic.
She lived way back in time,
In a cave where dragons used to climb.
She had no death
And she was like Lady Macbeth.

Lots of men took heart for her,
But not Sir Lancelot, no, no sir.
She made a potion made out of children's toes,
When the men drank it, they went into a doze.

Bianca Kingdon O'Shea (10)
Dr South's CE Primary School

Dog

Lead-walker,
Tree-stalker,
Biscuit-cruncher,
Food-muncher,
Cat-chaser,
Field-racer,
Water-lapper,
Rabbit-scrapper,
Puddle-splasher,
Postman-gnasher!

Zoë Masters (10)
Dr South's CE Primary School

Slowly

Slowly the river meets the sea,
Slowly in the pod, grows the pea,
Slowly the flower reaches the sun,
Slowly the day has been dusted and done.

Slowly the sun goes, out comes the moon,
Slowly the light will go very soon.
Slowly out come owls, also bats,
Slowly the kitten turns into a cat.

Slowly once I was two, but now I am ten,
Slowly the sun comes out once again.
Slowly the spring has sprung and now it is summer,
Slowly and gradually life is much better.

Debbie Robertson (10)
Dr South's CE Primary School

My Pet

Race-runner
Food-beggar
Meat-eater
Cat-chaser
Rabbit-scrapper
Good-smeller
My-runner
My pet!

Courtney Bateman (10)
Dr South's CE Primary School

There Was A Young Man From Troy

There was a young man from Troy,
Who always loved to annoy,
He would go round town
In his elegant gown
And go round the streets to annoy.
And go round the streets to annoy.

There was a young man from Troy
Who always loved to annoy,
He would tease people about their looks,
He would tease people how they hung their clothes on hooks,
And go round the streets to annoy.
And go round the streets to annoy.

Louisa Goodfellow (9)
Dr South's CE Primary School

Slowly

Slowly the river meets the sea,
Slowly the tide comes up to me,
Slowly the seaweed floats to land,
Slowly the crabs sink in the sand.

Slowly the hands move round the clock,
Slowly the crows begin to flock,
Slowly the light begins to fade,
The birds bed down in the leafy glade.

Lucy Brown (10)
Dr South's CE Primary School

Poetry

P oetry is good for me,
O melettes are brilliant for tea,
E nglish is hard for my friend Lee,
T rees are good for hiding a key,
R hubarb and custard attracts a bee,
Y achts are great for sailing the sea.

God help me, I can't stop writing poetry!

Amy Marie Billington (9)
Dr South's CE Primary School

Louisa

There was a girl called Louisa
Who was a dreadful teaser.
She got her brother
And tickled her mother,
The horrible girl called Louisa.

Claire Appleton (10)
Dr South's CE Primary School

Old Dog From Devon

There was an old dog from Devon,
He died and got transported to Heaven.
He followed a smell,
Which led him to Hell
And he was barbecued black by eleven!

Thomas Foxom (10)
Dr South's CE Primary School

THE GINGER CAT

Mucky-eater,
House-keeper,
Window-looker,
Lap-sitter,
Bed-sharer,
Mouse-eater,
Wind-runner,
Gaze-watcher,
Cat-fighter,
Loud-purrer,
Food-sharer,
Night-sleeper,
Naughty-fighter.

Melissa Murphy (9)
Dr South's CE Primary School

FATHER CHRISTMAS

Father Christmas rocks the house, he rocks the house.
He climbs down the chimney and the ladder snaps, snaps,
He falls on the fire and burns his rear.
He climbs back up and gets his sleigh into gear,
Then he disappears right out of here
To go and get some beer,
Then he'll cheer, 'A Happy New Year.'

A granny came along and got in my sleigh,
I said, 'I'll give you a motorbike, OK?
A yellow one with a sidecar, for my pet tarantula.'
Now that my story's coming to an end,
I'll give you a gift to blend.

Ben Allan (10)
Ducklington CE Primary School

Swimming Fever

All the people in the swimming pool
playing with their little ones,
fit men and women racing up and down,
diving under, splashes children make.

Splash! Splish! Splash! Splish!

Swish, swish! Went the mums.
Splash! Went the kids.

All the people in the swimming pool
playing with their little ones,
fit men and women racing up and down,
diving under, splashes children make.

Splash! Splish! Splash! Splish!

Swish, swish! Went the mums.
Splash! Went the kids.
Whoosh! Went the dads, doing a bomb.
'Brrr, brrr,' said the people coming out of the swimming pool.

Abigail Rimington (10)
Ducklington CE Primary School

Bonfire Night

Coming out to play by the fire's side,
Sparks and smoke rising into the night,
Small logs are being thrown onto the light,
It's Bonfire Night, it's Bonfire Night.

Watching pretty fireworks shooting to the sky,
A man goes to light them and then they fly.
Up they go into the clouds, ever so high,
It's Bonfire Night, it's Bonfire Night.

Sweeping up the leaves, into the fire they go,
Grabbing them all before the strong winds blow,
Jumping in a pile of them, up they throw,
It's Bonfire Night, it's Bonfire Night.

Laura Hughes (9)
Ducklington CE Primary School

THE MAGIC BOX

(Based on 'Magic Box' by Kit Wright)

I will put in my box . . .
The sound of dolphins singing,
A scent from a blood-red lily,
The taste of fresh snow falling from the sky.

I will put in my box . . .
The cry of a newborn baby,
A flap from the last dodo
And colour from new grass.

I will put in my box . . .
A horn from a unicorn,
A magical feather from a griffin
And magic from an enchantress' fingers.

I will put in my box . . .
A calming dream,
A baby's first kick
And a sigh from a mother.

My box is fashioned from fear and desire,
With moons on the front and good and evil in the corners.
I shall ride my box as though a horse
And find myself on an island full of hope.

Natali Garcia (10)
Ducklington CE Primary School

In My Madhouse

In my madhouse
We have a little mouse
And what a lot of fuss do the family make.
'Eek!' squealed Mum,
'Shoo!' shouted Dad,
While the maid's in the kitchen trying to bake.
In my madhouse,
We have a little mouse
And what a lot fuss do the family make.
'Ow!' squeaked sister,
'Eek!' squealed Mum,
'Shoo!' shouted Dad,
While the maid's in the kitchen trying to bake.
In my madhouse
We have a little mouse
And what a lot of fuss do the family make.
'Cool!' said brother,
'Ow!' squealed sister,
'Eek!' squealed Mum,
'Shoo!' shouted Dad,
While the maid's in the kitchen trying to bake.
Oh! While the maid's in the kitchen trying to bake.

Kirsty Hudson (9)
Ducklington CE Primary School

School's Out!

Schooldays go from Monday to Friday!
There are some noises money can't buy.
Drip, drip, goes the tap,
'Yeehaw!' said the chap.
'No! No!' said the teacher.
'Please! Please!' said the creature.

Today it's Friday, school's out,
Children always laugh and shout!
'Gossip, gossip!' said the kid,
'Ow! That hit my eyelid!'
Now it's finally five past three,
The end of school, yippee!

Melissa Wilmshurst (10)
Ducklington CE Primary School

The Fat Prince Of Peru

The fat Prince of Peru
Went to the zoo.
'Sssssss,' said the snake,
'Honk, honk,' said the goose,
For the animals were the finest in the land.

The fat Prince of Peru
Went to the zoo.
'Arh, arh,' said the monkey,
'Honk, honk,' said the goose,
'Sssssss,' said the snake,
For the animals were the finest in the land.

The fat Prince of Peru
Went to the zoo.
'Roar, roar,' said the tiger,
'Arh, arh,' said the monkey,
'Honk, honk,' said the goose,
'Sssssss,' said the snake,
For the animals were the finest in the land,
Oh! For the animals were the finest in the land,
Oh! For the animals were the finest in the land.

Karima Elouath (10)
Ducklington CE Primary School

HOLIDAY

Playing on the beach
Under the sun.
When we're at school,
We don't have much fun.

Dad and Mum are at work,
It's a long day for them.
My brother's being a jerk,
Come home from work.

Stressed out as usual,
Need some rest,
Need another holiday,
We're not at our best.

Playing on the beach,
Under the sun.
When we're at school
We don't have as much fun.
Oh! We don't have as much fun!

Joanna Dennis (9)
Ducklington CE Primary School

ME AND THE WEALTHY MAN

I was riding round the palace
On my little speckled horse,
In my dress of blue satin,
With a sprig of yellow gorse.

When I spied a wealthy man.
'Hello, my pretty maid,' said he.
'Hello, my good Sir,' said I.
'May I escort thee?'

He took me to his home so grand,
Five minutes in, he took my hand.
Five weeks later, here I am
With six fat babies and a pot of steaming ham!

Annie Rudd (9)
Ducklington CE Primary School

The Young Prince Of Peru

The young Prince of Peru
Had a big orchestra
And you never heard an orchestra like that before.
Honk, honk, went the saxophone,
Squeak, squeak, went the recorder
And the saxophone and the recorder
Were the finest in the land.
The young Prince of Peru
Had a big orchestra
And you never heard an orchestra like that before.
Bong, bong, went the drum,
Honk, honk, went the saxophone,
Squeak, squeak, went the recorder
And the recorder and the saxophone
Were the finest in the land.
The young Prince of Peru
Had a big orchestra
And you never heard an orchestra like that before.
Shake, shake, went the shakers,
Bong, bong, went the drum,
Honk, honk, went the saxophone,
Squeak, squeak, went the recorder
And the saxophone and the recorder
Were the finest in the land.

Oliver Cox (11)
Ducklington CE Primary School

SCHOOLDAY'S OUT

Schooldays start on Monday and end on Friday.
These are the noises that they made on Wednesday,
They go like this:
'Whaa, whaa, whaa . . .' said the little baby,
'Help, help, help . . .' said the bullies,
'Argh . . .' said the sillies
And it all comes out like a bad headache.
Here comes a head teacher and
These are the noises that he made:
'Walk, don't run,' said the headmaster,
'Or your legs will come off - so walk!'
'Ha, ha, ha,' said the children
And when it was three,
They all went home
With a big *woohoo!*

Ceri Brown (9)
Ducklington CE Primary School

MY LIFE!

When I was one, I was very dumb,
When I was two, my shoes were new,
When I was three, I climbed a tree,
When I was four, I opened a door,
When I was five, I went to a jive,
When I was six, my drinks were mixed,
When I was seven, I wanted to go to Heaven,
When I was eight, I was always late,
When I was nine, I had a fine,
When I was ten, I fed a hen,
Now I'm eleven, I really want to be seven!

Hannah Bishop (9)
Ducklington CE Primary School

INDIAN SONG

If I were to sing out to the stars
All the eagles would fly . . .
And if I woke in the midnight hours
I'd hear the wolf a-cry, a-cry!
I'd hear the wolf a-cry!

When the moon shines its silver haze
I lie down under the night . . .
Never sleeping; there to gaze
Just till the morning light, morn light!
Just till morning light!

I cannot help but croak to the frogs
And gabble away to the ducks . . .
Snorting and grunting to wild hogs
Some people think I'm nuts, I'm nuts!
Some people think I'm nuts!

Civilisation is far away,
Electricity's out of reach . . .
So I sing away the day
Lying on the beach, the beach!
Lying on the beach!

I howl with the wolves and play my drum,
Rain-dancing round and round . . ,
Testing the wind I lick my thumb,
There is prey to be found, be found!
There is prey to be found!

Hard day's work is done, time for sleep,
As the fire dies to ashes . . .
And the final darkness creeps,
Thunder rumbles, lightning flashes, flashes!
A new night is born with flashes!

Cressida Peever (10)
Ducklington CE Primary School

My Uncle's Song

My uncle's last name is Hell
And he lives in a red hotel.

He's entered a competition
And turned it into a mission, mission, mission.

He practised singing like mad,
But to be honest he was really bad
And he asked for help from my dad,
Which made him really glad.

And now he is a superstar,
Driving and playing his guitar
And this is the song he wrote . . .

'My last name is Hell
And I live in a red hotel,
La, la, la, la, la, la, la,
La, la, la, la, la, la, la!'

Ellen Hopkins (9)
Ducklington CE Primary School

Musical Sounds

When I hear the flute being played,
I think of birds
flying all around,
I hear the herds
grazing the ground.

When I hear the drums being played,
I think of elephants
stomping around.
I hear the ants
stamping the ground.

When I hear the piano being played,
I think of a concert.
Can you hear the concert?
Can you hear the piano being played?

Sarah Moir (10)
Ducklington CE Primary School

AUTUMN

Red and orange, the autumn leaves,
Falling down through the trees,
Making carpets soft to feel,
Under trees where I love to kneel.

See the asters in full bloom
Every single afternoon.
Soon we shall light the fire
And watch the flames leaping higher.

See the fruits the trees do bear,
Apple, damson, nut and pear.
Feel the dark and gloomy mist,
Holding the forest in its fist.

Can you smell the bonfire smoke?
Careful, it may make you choke!
Can you see the flames so bright
And people's faces flicker in the light?

Can you feel the wind so cool
Making ripples on the pool?
Can you see the waving trees
Rustling gently in the breeze?

Connie Jacobs (10)
Ewelme CE Primary School

My Extraordinary School

At my school there are four classes,
Mr Skinny's, Mrs Fat's,
Mr Bone's and Mrs Flesh's
And the headmaster is Mr Magic.

The school building is amazing.
An old crooked house,
Haunted and spooky,
With spiralling staircases.

The lessons are the best,
Flying and magic,
Chocolate making,
Spells and potions.

The light is of candles
Illuminating every room.
The heat is of fires,
Which blaze lovely and warm.

For clubs there are some weird things,
Cauldron stirring for instance,
Or wizard training
And sometimes tricks.

That's what happens at my school,
Such strange things.
Could I ask what happens at yours?
Maybe the teachers are aliens!

Elizabeth Spence (8)
Ewelme CE Primary School

Seasons

Summer
The smell of one million flowers,
The sound of a hummingbird,
The colour of a rose just bloomed,
Summer please come soon.

Spring
The smell of a dozen perfumes,
The sound of new life,
The colour of a beautiful rainbow,
Spring where are you?

Autumn
The smell of fresh, cold air,
The sound of the crunching of leaves,
The colour of a dull day,
Autumn what are you?

Winter
The smell of a cold breeze,
The sound of children playing in the snow,
The colour of a pure white rose,
Winter, see you soon.

The seasons are all different
Who would disagree with that?
Because spring is warm, summer is hot,
Autumn is chilly and winter is cold.

Lucinda Kenrick (9)
Ewelme CE Primary School

WHAT AM I?

Fast as a cheetah,
Slow as a snail,
Swift as the wind,
Pretty as a flower,
Quiet as a mouse,
Loud as an elephant.
Can you guess?
Because I am a bird.

Faron Watts (10)
Ewelme CE Primary School

THE STEALTHY TIGER

An animal with eyes of stealth,
Fur like stripy silk.
His teeth are deadly daggers.
He slips away in the black of midnight.

James Harber (8)
Ewelme CE Primary School

FRIEND

F riendship is the strongest thing,
R emember friends are always there,
I f you're lonely, they're always within,
E verybody around you,
N o one can be a true enemy,
D o you believe in an everlasting friendship?

Jessica Veitch (11)
Ewelme CE Primary School

THE READER OF THIS POEM

(Based on 'The Writer Of This Poem' by Roger McGough)

The reader of this poem . . .
Is as cracked as white chalk
As daft as a joke
As mucky as a bog.

As troublesome as mums
As brash as a king
As bouncy as a rubber ball
As quiet as a dog.

As sneaky as a fox
As tappy-toe as a good swing band
As empty as the universe
As echoey as loud children in a gym hall.

As bossy as a teenage sister
As prickly as a pair
Of socks made out of thistles
And tigers' teeth.

As vain as an extremely rich snob
As boring as an old headmaster
As smelly as the kitchen drain
Outside the sewage works.

As hungry as a lion
That feeds upon a zebra
As gasping as your teacher
As gotcha as a ghoul.

As fruitless as a cake of gunge
As creeping up as a sly old dad
The reader of this poem, I hope
Knows how to take a joke!

Jack Ventress (9)
Ewelme CE Primary School

THE DINOSAURS WHO ATE OUR SCHOOL

The day the dinosaurs came to call,
They gobbled the gate, the playground wall
And slate by slate the roof an' all
The staffroom, gym and the hall
And classrooms, giant or small.
So,

They're absolutely great,
They're mega, mega cool.
The dinosaurs who gobbled,
The dinosaurs who gobbled,
The dinosaurs who gobbled our school.

Pupils screamed, teachers ran
They swooped at them with a big wingspan.
They slew a few and then began,
To chew through a policeman,
Parked car and transit van.
Wow!

They're absolutely great,
They're mega, mega cool.
The dinosaurs who gobbled,
The dinosaurs who gobbled,
The dinosaurs who gobbled our school.

They bit off the head of the Head,
They weren't sad that she was dead.
'Poor Ted,' said Deputy Head, Ned,
The dinosaurs fed, their mouths were red,
As they swallowed next the PE shed.
Ohh!

They're absolutely great,
They're mega, mega cool.
The dinosaurs who gobbled,
The dinosaurs who gobbled,
The dinosaurs who gobbled our school.

It's thanks to them we've been freed,
We won't write, we needn't read.
Me and my mates all agreed,
We're very pleased with them indeed,
So clear the way let them proceed,
Cos!

They're absolutely great,
They're mega, mega cool.
The dinosaurs who gobbled,
The dinosaurs who gobbled,
The dinosaurs who gobbled our school.

Elliott Hughes (10)
Ewelme CE Primary School

What Is She Like?

This person is a cushion,
She reminds me of fur,
Her colour is soft yellow,
She reminds me of a cheerful bird.
She is a clever cat,
A kind mum,
The element of Earth
And she would like a swan
To be dedicated to her when she dies.

Elspeth Walker (8)
Ewelme CE Primary School

Will You?

Will you love me if I love you?
Will you dance if I dance too?
Will you smile if I smile as well?
Will you agree to the wedding bell?

Will you miss me if I go away?
Will you hug me every day?
Will you sing if I sing along?
Will the words be right or wrong?

Will you help me when my world falls apart?
Will you heal my broken heart?
Will you still look at me with loving eyes?
Will you comfort me when someone dies?

Will you treat me with kindness and grace?
Will you still love my changing face?
Will you still love me when I'm old and grey,
Or will you leave and go away?

Will you share my life forever?
Will you cherish me, hurt me never?
Will you walk with me down the aisle,
Make me yours, share my smile?

So, will you?

Ellie Clements (10)
Ewelme CE Primary School

Stars Cinquain

Gentle
Sparkling sight
Making pictures all night
Illuminating the dark sky
Precious

Twinkle
Shimmering bright
Like a red-hot firelight
Glistening as the night goes by
A dream.

Hannah Fitzgerald (10)
Ewelme CE Primary School

The Reader Of This Poem

(Based on 'The Writer Of This Poem' by Roger McGough)

The reader of this poem . . .
Is as cracked as ice
As daft as a duck
As mucky as a baby

As troublesome as a monster
As brash as a broom
As bouncy as a pogo stick
As quiet as a rabbit

As sneaky as a witch
As tappy toe as jazz
As empty as a bone
As echoey as, as, as, as

As bossy as a big sister
As prickly as a pear
An elephant made out of glue and stones
As vain as water
As boring as a cow
As smelly as a pig
Outside the kitchen door.

Hayley Jameson (8)
Ewelme CE Primary School

TALENTS

Everybody has talent,
It's just hiding.
If you look for it,
Your talent will come and find you.
Whether it's singing, dancing or writing,
Art, poetry or playing musical instruments,
If you share your talent,
You'll end up getting more.

Don't give up looking for your talent,
For you'll never find it if you do.
If you keep on looking hard,
You'll soon meet your gifts.
If others say you're not good,
Don't listen! Keep on trying,
Believe in your talent,
You'll end up getting more!

Don't let yourself get teased about your ambition,
Rise above it and believe in yourself.
Talents bring you pleasure and satisfaction,
Talents are things you can improve on,
A talent is a gift from God to men,
Other people enjoy listening to and watching your talents,
Use your talent wisely,
You'll end up getting more!

Bella Maine (9)
Ewelme CE Primary School

TIMES

Time flies in a flash
Fun times gone and past
Boring times go so slow
Like a journey in a bus

Scary times
Fun times
Wicked times
Bad times

Times of worship
Times of peace
Times of thinking
Times of release

Times to pray
Every day
Times to play
Each day

Time to sleep
Time to relax
Time to cry
Time to smile

There is a time for everything
In each and every way.

Trudy Jones (10)
Ewelme CE Primary School

THE YEAR

Here comes Spring
In her green cloak,
Sprinkles the gardens
With primroses and daisies.

Then comes Summer,
In her plum-red blouse,
Bringing sun and
Thunder clouds.

Next comes Autumn
In her golden dress,
Swaps the leaves
For juicy fruit.

Last comes Winter,
Covering the ground with her fur coat,
Invites the hail, snow and wind.
Another year has come and gone.

Elspeth Wilson (9)
Ewelme CE Primary School

DARK WOLF

Dark wolf is like a shadow,
Always there when you feel bad,
Soon vanishes when you make up.
Dark wolf is like misery,
Grief, sadness, desolation.
Dark wolf represents iniquity and evil
And he comes when you fall out.

Daniel Miles (9)
Ewelme CE Primary School

ANIMALS

Birds flying
As thunder comes.

Cows collapse as the
Cold winter comes.

Dogs bark as hailstones
Tap in all places.

Pigs squeal
As sun rises.

Sheep are white
As snow falls.

Ducks quack as
Water becomes ice.

Jonathan Lansley (10)
Ewelme CE Primary School

WIND

Wind is like a person,
Spinning round and round,
It growls like a wolf,
Howls like a hound,
It smashes against trees
And many other things,
Flying around the world,
You may think it has wings,
It gushes in the treetops, it sings in the sky,
It speaks to you in whispers,
But no one knows why.

Rosie Duffield (10)
Ewelme CE Primary School

I LIKE . . .

I like smooth things, warm and cuddly,
You like rough things, lumpy and hard.

I like to relax when the sun shines brightly,
You like to play in the dull, dark rain.

I like butter, smooth and slippery,
You like Ryvita, bumpy and solid.

I like hamsters, cute and friendly,
You like snakes, scaly and fierce.

I like violins, soft and gentle,
You like drums, loud and booming.

All of these things are opposites,
But what we like makes us different.

Grace Toland (10)
Ewelme CE Primary School

TIGER

In the depths of a steamy jungle
Creeping stealthily through the vines and grasses
He has dazzling eyes and bold-coloured stripes
You would know him if you saw him,
It's the tiger.
His icy cold glare gives his enemies a fright,
It's a good thing too, he's everybody's enemy.
He despises the humans,
They took away his home,
They took away his cubs,
They took away his wife
And now they are coming for him . . .

Charlie Walker (11)
Ewelme CE Primary School

Summer

In summer all the grass is green,
the flowers bloom red and yellow.
The sun shines and the wind isn't mean.

The days are longer
and the nights are shorter,
the sun is stronger.

People have days out
to the beach and parks,
children have fun, they laugh and shout.

Summer is the best season,
come and join us,
there is no reason.

Laura Griffin (9)
Ewelme CE Primary School

My Friend

My skin is light, hers is dark,
My hair is blonde, hers is black,
My eyes are blue, hers are brown,
I live in a house, she lives in a hut,
I have one brother, she has four,
I have two dogs, she has five,
I have rain, she has sun,
I believe in one god, she believes in several,
I go to school by bus, she walks,
I live in England, she lives in Africa,
We may be worlds apart
But we're the best of
Friends.

Jessica Craven-Todd (11)
Ewelme CE Primary School

My World

In my world everything is made out of sweets,
The cups of tea are daffodils,
My green garden is made out of green Smarties,
My really good, comfy mattress is made out of Turkish Delight,
The local lake is made out of runny melted chocolate,
The seats in the park are made out of fruit pastilles.

Whistles are made out of lolly whistles,
People are made out of chocolate bars,
Money is chocolate coins,
Birds' eggs are Cadbury's Creme Eggs,
Fabric is rice paper,
The snow is icing,
The Colosseum in Rome is made out of Whirl Winders
And that's what's in my head!

Amelia Halhead (9)
Ewelme CE Primary School

Autumn

Autumn is a time when the weather is gloomy and cold,
Autumn is a time when the trees are bare and old.
Autumn is a time when the leaves fall off the trees,
Autumn is a time when the branches sway in the breeze.

Autumn is a time when the leaves are red and brown,
Autumn is a time when the leaves come tumbling down.
Autumn is a time when bonfires are alight,
Autumn is a time when we have long dark nights.
Autumn!

Gemma Bolton (10)
Ewelme CE Primary School

WHAT IS THE WIND?

The wind is a draught
From under the door,
It makes you cold
As it blows all around you,
It can turn water to ice
On a cold winter morning,
In winter it's so cold
You start to shiver,
In summer it's a cool breeze.

It can howl like a wolf,
It can whisper like a tiny child,
It can hoot like an owl
It can cry like a baby,
It can whistle like a train.

The wind howls round ancient trees
And makes them crash to the ground.
Doors bang.
Windows rattle.
Kites soar high in the sky
And dance with the clouds.
Grass sways with the breeze
And rivers rush to the sea.

Fiery-coloured leaves float down
Like snow into drifts,
But we feel warm and cosy
Indoors.
Sometimes I like the wind.

Louise Wells (8)
Ewelme CE Primary School

My Best Friend

My best friend has long, curly ears,
His tail is small and stumpy.
His eyes are the darkest brown
And when you look into them,
It's like a very deep ocean.

When I come home from school,
He's excited that I'm there.
He welcomes me home
And wags his tail.

I love to take my friend out,
We run, we play ball, sometimes he hides.
We always have fun.
I'm never lonely with my friend.

When we arrive home,
We share the sofa.
I stroke Buster, my best friend,
Everything is very peaceful.

Jack Eccles (10)
Ewelme CE Primary School

Holding The Baby

I felt embarrassed, because she kept looking at me, as if I was her mum.

My lap got warm from her nappy and I tried to hold my nose.

She was making me feel uncomfortable, because every time I put her in a place she moved into a different place.

She kept irritating me because she kept making
funny noises and blowing bubbles.

Her legs kept kicking me and giving me bruises
and touching my face with her tiny toes.

I didn't like holding the baby.

Brogan West (9)
Longcot & Fernham Primary School

In Sixty Years

In sixty years' time when I am sixty-eight
I will tell my grandchildren about:

Drive-in movies where you used to park your cars
and watch movies.

About the day out at the White Horse Show
watching the Jack Russell racing.

About sponsored walks with school
up White Horse Hill.

About the time I went on holiday and a
coconut fell on my auntie's toe.

About the special events at school like the
Christmas productions and Golden Jubilee
Celebration.

About the time when we went to Wimbourne
and a seagull came down and pinched my chip.

About the time when my mum jumped over
a hay bale and broke her foot.

Maxwell Jackson (9)
Longcot & Fernham Primary School

The Monster Under My Bed

One night I couldn't get to sleep,
so I looked under my bed and had a peep.
I saw an ugly monster with sharp white teeth
and a hairy, purple belly underneath.
Then I heard the monster say,
'Please can I come out and play?'
So in the middle of the night,
we went and had a pillow fight.
We made a mess of all my toys,
the monster made an awful noise.
I heard my mum outside the door,
so I quickly tidied up the floor.
She opened the door and took a look,
I was in my bed reading a book.

David Cole (9)
Longcot & Fernham Primary School

How To Make A School

To make a perfect school we need
some classrooms as big as the sky,
with teachers as happy as clowns.
We also need some children
as bright as the sun,
with a field as wide as a jungle,
with chairs as comfy as cotton wool.
The heating as warm as a roaring fire,
classrooms as colourful as a rainbow,
dinners as tasty as a real chef's cooking
and last of all we need a headmistress
as pretty as a princess.

Sophie Hingston (8)
Longcot & Fernham Primary School

Exciting Sea Moments

The sea is full of great things,
Sometimes it sings.
Listen to its raging waves,
It will show you the way to save.
The sea is full of great things,
Sometimes it sings.

The sea can make crazy sounds,
Sounds like a load of hounds.
Feeling good, feeling careful,
Off it goes being cheerful.
The sea can make crazy sounds,
Sounds like a load of hounds.

The sea *swishes*, the sea *swoshes*,
Everyone's wearing their galoshes.
When it swerves,
It has a nerve.
The sea *swishes*, the sea *swoshes*,
Everyone's wearing their galoshes.

Gorgia Lisi (10)
Longcot & Fernham Primary School

The Tropical Rainforest

Howling wind hear me,
Dancing trees hail me,
Scary shadows be with me,
Booby traps don't trap me,
Crunchy grass do not crunch,
Rainforest be with me at all times.

Jordan Dowell (8)
Longcot & Fernham Primary School

My Life

I am a little hamster
Hammy is my name

My fur is soft and brown and white
And I always come out at night

Round and round in my wheel I run
I really think this is great fun

When Ben gets me out to play
We have different games each day

I roll around in my ball
And often bump into the wall

I nibble on my honey sticks
And when I move I'm very quick

I fill my pouches with my food
And eat it when I'm in the mood

Ben always has to clean my cage
This always seems to take an age

I haven't seen Ben at all today
He doesn't seem to want to play

Snuggled up deep inside my bed
I really am a sleepyhead

In my bed I've stayed all day
Hidden, hidden well away

I love my home, my toys, my play
I love my food and wish to stay

I hate it when they go away
Cos there's no one quite like Ben

So now I've told you how I feel
It was good to have that say

My hamster life is good and real
I'll tell you more some other day.

Ben Church (10)
Longcot & Fernham Primary School

THERE'S A MONSTER IN MY HOUSE

There's a monster in my house,
My mum says it's the central heating,
My dad says it's a mouse,
Others say it's a sheep bleating -
Somewhere in the hills
But you can never see him
Cos he's always very still.

There's a monster in my house,
Living down the stair,
I know he's not a mouse,
Cos I'm sure I've seen him there.
He hides my socks and underwear,
So I know he's about somewhere.

There's a monster in my house,
Always sleeping in the day,
His best friend is a mouse
And I've heard them say,
We're not scary any day,
But we just like to scare you away.

Richard Mace (10)
Longcot & Fernham Primary School

The Football Match

Duthore V Ferndale

'OK now go to your positions. No Gary you're not in goal
you're in defence. Yes I now you like being in goal but you're not.
Anyway, Harry and Jason kick-off, no Harry not you and Greg.
Yes I know he's your best friend but, just get on with it.
OK now Greg pass it to Jason, yes! Pick it up Jason.
No! Not with your hands with your feet.
Yes Jason I know you don't know how to, it's just an expression.
Mark up lads, Gary! Stop marking Jack, mark someone on the
other team. Yes Gary I know you don't know anyone on the other
team . . . just *mark* someone.
OK lads if the ball comes to you, get it out of the penalty area.
Stop! Don't all go for the same ball . . . oh wait someone has to . . .
Nooo! 1-0.
We will need a miracle to get back in this. No Ryan you don't
have to pray. Let's kick-off again, we can get into this.
Yes finally we're in their half.
Ouch that's got to hurt, come on ref that was a foul.
OK Josh next time that happens just dive. No don't dive now,
he's only marking you.
Get back into position while he's taking the free kick.
Well I'm glad someone knows what position he's in.
Come on boys keep your heads up, no Gary don't look up that high,
you need to watch the players and watch out for the . . .
ouch! I felt that.'

After match team talk

'You were very lucky that Gary cracked the goalpost
or we would have been thrashed at least 10-0.

Yes Jack, we did lose and yes, it was by one goal.
Oh yes, by the way I've got something to tell you,
I'm resigning. No, don't cry, what was that Jack?
Oh, you're cheering.'

Patrick Archard (11)
Longcot & Fernham Primary School

THE SEA

I am so big, my body's blue,
I love playing with children and fish,
But I can be rough and dangerous too.
I'm popular with all the lovely sea creatures
And many playful humans.

My long waves on my long back,
Dolphins, diving, leaping gracefully,
Sharks and whales spying on their prey
And it is easy as 1, 2, 3, swallow and gulp
As the fish has gone.

I eat, I curve, I bend all over,
I swallow and gulp whole ships and treasure,
I feel so angry and ashamed,
Another ship has sunk and people are lost.

But also I feel popular because:
In my bottom I have sharks and whales eating,
Fish floating,
Dolphins jumping, leaping and curving.

Amy Cooper (10)
Longcot & Fernham Primary School

MINE, MY MUM AND DAD'S JOBS

My dad says he's a plumber,
Bending pipes to fit,
But I think he's Superman,
I found his tights in the basket.

My mum says she's a teacher,
Giving people tests,
But I think she's a secret agent,
Because I found her bullet-proof vests.

My family think I'm a schoolboy,
With books and books to fill,
But I am in the army,
With a licence to kill.

Robert Law (9)
Longcot & Fernham Primary School

THE TWIN TOWERS

It was busy with people rushing around,
Footsteps like elephants shake the ground,
A shadowy figure looked up in the sky
And saw an aeroplane that wasn't passing by;
It was coming towards this place
And smashed it down before the race.
There was running and screaming for ten seconds flat
And under the rubble, belongings were sat,
But nothing except stillness came and went,
Through those few last moments the last breath was spent.

Sophie Iredale (10)
Longcot & Fernham Primary School

If I Were A Bird

If I were a bird I would fly the many seas
And swoop and glide through the greenest of trees.
If I were a bird I would glide through crimson skies
And catch the thermals with which to rise.

If I were a bird I would perform many tricks,
Loop-the-loops through obstacles of trees, twigs and sticks.
If I were a bird I would tease next door's cat,
By hovering and tweeting above where it sat.

If I were a bird I would fly to faraway lands
And fly to the many concerts played by my favourite bands.
If I were a bird I would fly over the country scenes
And try to find what this life means.

Ashley Payne (10)
Longcot & Fernham Primary School

Winter

The snow falls,
Water freezes,
Children play,
Snowflakes fall,
Ice breaks,
Snowmen being built,
Snowballs being thrown,
Rain falls,
Wind blows,
Snow thaws.

Claire Stallard (10)
Longcot & Fernham Primary School

The Moon's Kingdom

The Moon dances across the sky,
Ruling her kingdom as time goes by.
Some obey her violet rap,
Others just shoot away into the black.

She rules all the stars the galaxy holds,
But dislikes the comets, they're too quick to control.

Her successor, the Sun, he helps her a lot,
Her prime is something called solar eclipse,
When the Earth looks on as she blacks out the Sun.

She likes her kingdom velvety-black,
So she hides when the dawn breaks,
She's such a scaredy-cat!

So if it is darkish tonight,
Look out of the window,
You might see a full moon in flight.

Amy Thomas (10)
Longcot & Fernham Primary School

My Grandpa

My grandpa is as busy as an ant,
My grandpa is as quiet as a mouse,
My grandpa is as tall as five tables on top of each other.
My grandpa wears clothes as nice as a king,
My grandpa is as warm as a fire.
I love my grandpa as much as he is.

Ruth Cooper (8)
Longcot & Fernham Primary School

My Diet

For breakfast I have honey,
I spread it with a knife,
There is no need to worry,
I've done it all my life!

For lunch I have baked beans,
A whole tin by myself,
It gives me a little bit of wind,
But it's very good for my health!

For tea I have marshmallows,
Marshmallows on a stick,
I know it's not hygienic,
But they're very nice to lick!

For supper I have chocolate cake,
It's very nice to eat,
The problem with my diet is
I cannot see my feet!

Michael Cole (11)
Longcot & Fernham Primary School

The Exam

Excellent pencil, tell me,
Wonderful paper, guide me,
Exam teacher, help me.
As the time flies by our exam is up,
Fantastic teacher tell me if I've passed.

Nia Richards (8)
Longcot & Fernham Primary School

FUN BALLET

In my ballet class
we do points
point, spring, point.

In my ballet class
we do jumps
jump, hop, jump.

In my ballet class
we do skips
skip, leap, skip.

In my ballet class
I have fun
fun, fun, fun.

Alice McNamara (8)
Longcot & Fernham Primary School

THE HAUNTED SCROLL

In my loft I found a scroll
And the story on it was about a mole.
I put it in my wooden chest,
But last night it came alive and was a pest.
It woke me up
And as I startled I smashed my bedside cup.
I told it to go away,
But all it said was, 'I want to stay!'
In the morning Mum yelled you see,
I tried to tell her it wasn't me.
That's how the haunted scroll began.

Naomi Lisi (10)
Longcot & Fernham Primary School

PONY CLUB DAY

'Hello everyone my name is May,
Welcome to Pony Club Day.
Just tell me your names quick,
Come on the clock's going *tick, tick.*
Chloe and Clara,
Rupert and Tara,
Sam and Tia,
Tilly and Mia,
Now I'll tell you your pony,
But no moaning,
Chloe and Clara you're on Rosie and Lilly,
Rupert and Tara you're on Poppy and Billy,
Sam and Tia you're on Marble and Bobbin,
Tilly and Mia you're on Prince and Robin.
Go and get a grooming box, chip chop,
No Tara you can't go on Hip Hop.
Right everyone pick up a body brush,
Come on Sam we're in a rush,
Brush the tail just like I am,
Quickly, move back Sam.
Oops it was a direct hit,
Here are some clothes get changed quick,
Now put on your pony's tack,
We're going on a hack.
Come on Tia, smack Bobbin hard,
Let's have a canter to get back to the yard.
Untack your pony really fast,
For it's very nearly half-past.
Yes Mrs Goody they were a delight,
But the accident with Sam gave me quite a fright!'

Anna Blesing (10)
Longcot & Fernham Primary School

POLO

We've got a dog called Polo,
That everyone can see,
She doesn't play with anyone,
Just with the family.

She sleeps on my bed,
Right next to my head.
Sometimes she smells
And sometimes she yells.

Polo plays with her ball,
She comes when she's called.
She's often dirty and wet,
But she is still our pet.

Sometimes she yaps
And sometimes she flaps,
But she is our love
And as gentle as a dove.

Matthew Harris (11)
Longcot & Fernham Primary School

THE SNOWSTORM

At the start the grass was green,
At the end it could not be seen.
The snowflakes came down twirling and light,
Making the ground all frosty and white.

The winds were icy when they began to blow,
The land lay cold under its blanket of snow.
The silent shivers crept across the ground,
Throughout the land there was not a sound.

James Heathcote (9)
Longcot & Fernham Primary School

A Long, Lazy Summer's Day

Summer is when the sun shines.
White fluffy clouds in the sky.
Butterflies fluttering from flower to flower,
Bees buzzing busily collecting pollen.
Cows grazing in the fields,
A cat sleeping in the shade of a tree.
Tractors working in the fields,
As the days grow shorter and cooler as autumn approaches.

Sarah Stallard (10)
Longcot & Fernham Primary School

Space

Moon
The moon is our night-light
Silently gleaming bright
It has a gravitational pull
Which I think is cool.

Sun
The sun is bright and hot
The sound is crackle and pop
It will fry you in one second flat
So let's hope you have some fat.

Pluto
Pluto is made of ice
Your ear drums will not stay nice
There is no squawking here
So it is much to fear.

Samuel Ward (10)
Marcham CE Primary School

Noises In The Kitchen

I hear the *dripping* of the tap
The *roaring* of the gas
The tumble dryer *rumbling* away
Sloshing of our drinks
The *grinding* of the pepper mill as the corns
are ground to dust
The *humming* of the fridge and
The *sizzling* of the sausages
Finally, the *scraping* of chairs as we begin to leave.

Joseph Cauchi (10)
Marcham CE Primary School

A Day At A Swimming Pool

A single shriek,
The whistles of a lifeguard,
Children chatting wildly,
Someone coughing and spluttering,
A man moving slickly and silently
Through the water,
The echoing of the wall.

Thomas Horne (11)
Marcham CE Primary School

Cymbals

Cymbals are the latest craze
Our class are going through a phase
Crashes, clangs, bangs and *booms*
Are all you hear when you enter the room

The teacher asks us to quieten down
But all we do is clown around
Clangs and *bashes* louder than before
Our teacher's ears are really sore.

Hannah Fathers (10)
Marcham CE Primary School

The Sound Walk

A soft bang in the sky
Some birds chirping on the yellow wall
Loud music vibrating in the wind
The windy rustle of the trees
Rabbits banging their feet on the cold, leafy floor
Squirrels jumping from tree to tree
Children giggling, parents yelling
Suddenly silence, I can hear the wind blow again.

Stephanie Andrews (10)
Marcham CE Primary School

Listen To The Sounds Around

The sound of children's laughter,
A firework display,
These are some of the things
That I have heard today.
If you hear noise streaming through the air,
Listen to what they say
And you will enjoy your day.

Steven Keen (11)
Marcham CE Primary School

Crash, Bang, Bash!

At first all is quiet,
No rustles from the leaves,
All we hear is silence,
Until someone screams.

Crash, bang, bash!

That sounded like an orchestra,
With everyone out of key,
It really was quite frightful,
You should come and see.

Crash, bang, bash!

Here we go again,
But this time it's much worse,
No crashing or bangs now,
It just won't all fit into one verse.

Crash, bang, bash!

Now it is really mad,
I scream and begin to run,
There's a herd of singing elephants,
Yelling my name as they come.

Crash, bang, bash, bash, bash!

Eleanor Mathews (10)
Marcham CE Primary School

School

A car went past, *zoom!*
Then scratching on the board, *squeak!*
Flowing pens on paper, *squiggle, squiggle!*
And the tapping of feet, *tip, tap!*

The chairs were scraping, *scrape, scrape!*
The erasers were clapping, *bang, bang!*
The children were counting, *one, two!*
And the teachers were chatting, *chit, chat!*

Joe Richardson (9)
Marcham CE Primary School

WHAT CAN YOU HEAR?

Listen, listen, what can you hear?
A tiny baby screaming through the land.
Listen, listen, what can you hear?
Waves crashing and smashing onto the rocks.
Listen, listen, what can you hear?
An angry dog barking and howling like a banshee.
Listen, listen, what can you hear?
The squeaking of chalk on the blackboard.

Tom Tierney (10)
Marcham CE Primary School

SCHOOL POEM

S is for school where we get our education
C is for communication when we are doing geography
H is for health when we are doing science
O is for octopus when we are doing animals
O is for oval when we are doing maths
L is for lifting when we are doing PE
! is for literacy when we are doing punctuation!

Jenny Fathers (8)
Marcham CE Primary School

HOUSE OF HELL

If you stand outside my house
It'll give you a terrible shock.
You won't want to walk in
Especially at 7 o'clock:

My younger sister will strut up
And take off your coat and hat,
Then she will dance and sing
In a voice completely flat.

If you run into the kitchen
Stifling a scream,
You'll find a cuddly baby
Wailing and chucking ice cream.

You'll find my mother cleaning up
Muttering under her breath
And reaching for an aspirin saying,
'I feel like death.'

If you wade through piles of newspaper
Thinking you've been here too long,
You'll find me waiting there
And I'll tell you where you went wrong.

Ellen H Walton (11)
Marcham CE Primary School

SITTING AT MY DESK

A car went past, *zoom,*
The kids were going *squeak,*
A ball outside went *boom*
And then the board went *creak.*

The teacher went on shouting,
The wind outside went *whooo!*
Half the class were counting,
As the bird sang, *cuckoo, cuckoo!*

Georgia Upjohn (10)
Marcham CE Primary School

The Scream Of Death

The scream of death is death itself,
It rustles through the leaves like a ghostly animal,
Then it ambushes the trees,
It whooshes up, flailing, trying to reach the sky.
Suddenly it bursts through the treetops into the darkness,
With a final petrifying scream it explodes.

Ruth Narramore (10)
Marcham CE Primary School

Drum Kits

Drum kits rock,
The latest craze,
They cause a racket
In different ways.

The bang of the snare,
A cymbal to hit,
I really love
My new drum kit.

James Logan (10)
Marcham CE Primary School

School

M orland are the best
A head of all the rest
R unning around in sport
C an we remember what we've been taught?
H andwriting we all hate
A ssemblies are great
M aths and literacy before our break

S ometimes we make a big mistake
C ooking in the kitchen
H opping around, sewing and stitching
O ther people in trouble
O ther people jump in puddles
L ife in school is cool.

Rebecca Rowe
Marcham CE Primary School

Whizz, Bang, Pop

The sudden screams of laughter
And then the cheerful chatter
Whoosh! There they go
With a *whizz,* a *bang* and a *pop!*

Then a sudden shriek
The witches are unleashed
They shoot into the sky
With a *rumble* and *crack*
Like lightning, then,
Whizz, bang, pop!

Jessie O'Higgins (11)
Marcham CE Primary School

My Cat Cleo

My cat Cleo sleeps a lot,
Usually on my bed.
She runs around the garden
Letting me stroke her head.
My cat Cleo loves to sleep,
Especially in her box.
She always, always needs to peep,
To see if there's a fox.
My cat Cleo has her tail up
And always loves to play.
But then she has to sleep again
And play another day.

Sophie Dyer (9)
Marcham CE Primary School

Sitting At My Desk

Scratching of chalk on the board,
Great giggles exploding behind me.
A roar of an aeroplane above,
A zooming car outside.
Buzz, buzz, buzz there's a bumblebee,
The teacher's counting, one, two, three.

Branches snapping as the wind blows,
Birds in the trees, *cheep, cheep*.
A woodpecker's tapping,
Everyone's shouting.
Rustling as a squirrel runs up a tree,
The teacher's *still* counting, 22, 23!

Kathleen Macnee (10)
Marcham CE Primary School

MY DOG ARTHUR

My dog Arthur is a lovely dog,
He plays with me all day,
Except when I go to school,
He always runs away.

Whenever I come home from school,
He wags his tail to say,
'Do you have to go again or could you stay and play?'

Arthur is a lovely dog,
A Labrador - he's black,
When it's raining outdoors,
He likes to wear his mac!

Chloe Hopgood (9)
Marcham CE Primary School

IN MY GARDEN

In my garden I am standing,
I listen to everything that I hear
I hear:
Birds *cheeping,*
Sister *giggling,*
Baby *splashing,*
Mummy *chatting,*
Rabbit *thumping,*
Music *banging.*

Quiet, now I can't hear anything.

Sandy Walker (10)
Marcham CE Primary School

Rascals

When you come into our class you'll hear:
Alexandria arguing,
Daisy drinking,
David drawing,
Eleanor eating,
Ellen entering,
Georgia giggling,
Hannah humming,
Henry hammering,
James jumping,
Jessica jigging,
Jessie juggling,
Joe joking,
Joseph jogging,
Kathleen kicking,
Philip pleading,
Ruth rhyming,
Samuel sighing,
Sandy singing,
Sophie sliding,
Stephanie shrieking,
Steven sleeping,
Tierney tripping,
Thomas tapping,
Tom tackling,
William whining
And Mrs Rook just says we're *rascals!*

Jessica Logan (10)
Marcham CE Primary School

SWEETS

S is for sherbet, that's colourful and nice.
W is for Willy Wonka's chocolate.
E is for eating lovely sweets.
E is for eclairs, chocolate and nice.
T is for Terry's Chocolate Orange.
S is for sherbet lemon.

Georgia Tolley (9)
Marcham CE Primary School

TEN MYSTERIOUS MICE

10 mysterious mice, drinking lots of wine
One got too drunk, then there were nine.
9 mysterious mice fishing with blue bait,
One fell in the river, then there were eight.
8 mysterious mice playing hide-and-seek with Kevin,
One tripped and grazed her knee, then there were seven.
7 mysterious mice stealing pic 'n' mix
One got caught by the shopkeeper, then there were six.
6 mysterious mice eating cheese and chive,
One got left in the cafe, then there were five.
5 mysterious mice trying to break the law,
One got arrested, then there were four.
4 mysterious mice drinking strong coffee and tea,
One choked on a sugar lump, then there were three.
3 mysterious mice watching Winnie the Pooh,
One went Tigger-mad, then there were two.
2 mysterious mice not having much fun,
One burst into tears, then there was one.
1 mysterious mouse singing in the rain,
He drowned in a puddle and was never seen again!

Ellie Boshell (9)
Millbrook Primary School

I Am A Mouse

I am a mouse
sneaking out my hole.

I am a mouse
searching for food.

I am a mouse
sniffing and sniffing.

I am a mouse,
I have just seen cheese.

I am a mouse,
squash!

I was a mouse
sneaking out my hole.

I was a mouse
searching for food.

I was a mouse
sniffing and sniffing.

I was a mouse
that had just seen cheese.

I was a mouse.

Scott James Hetherington (9)
Millbrook Primary School

TEN LAZY LEGOMEN

Ten lazy Legomen looking rather fine
one died of boredom, then there were nine.
Nine lazy Legomen, time is getting late,
one started snoring, then there were eight.
Eight lazy Legomen sleeping like heaven,
one wouldn't wake up so then there were seven.
Seven lazy Legomen eating chocolate Twix,
one ate far too much so then there were six.
Six lazy Legomen trying hard to stay alive,
one couldn't manage so then there were five.
Five lazy Legomen squashing through the door,
one burst by accident so then there were four.
Four lazy Legomen giggling with glee,
one was left giggling so then there were three.
Three lazy Legomen, all have got the flu,
one sneezed himself to Jupiter so then there were two.
Two lazy Legomen trying to lift a ton,
one let go and broke his arm so then there was one.
One lazy legoman sucking his thumb,
the poor man swallowed it so then there were none.

Mitchell Thomas (9)
Millbrook Primary School

GALLOPING HORSES

Ten galloping horses neighing in a line,
One fell and hit his head, then there were nine.
Nine galloping horses rushing for the gate,
One fell in a ditch, then there were eight.
Eight galloping horses rearing up to heaven,
One fell on its back, then there were seven.
Seven galloping horses running over sticks,
One fell and ripped her skirt, then there were six.
Six galloping horses jumping over a hive,
One got stung by a bee, then there were five.

Five galloping horses hitting their heads on a door,
One got knocked out, then there were four.
Four galloping horses climbing up a tree,
One lost its balance on a branch, then there were three.
Three galloping horses sitting on the loo,
One flushed himself down, then there were two.
Two galloping horses, they are nearly all gone,
One says he is tired, then there was one.
One galloping horse waiting to go home,
He got taken away, then there were none.

Robynne Armstrong (9)
Millbrook Primary School

TEN SKATING ELEPHANTS

Ten skating elephants all skating in a line,
one skated into a wall, then there were nine.
Nine skating elephants fell into the gate,
one broke his leg, then there were eight.
Eight skating elephants all in heaven,
one got lost, then there were seven.
Seven skating elephants all playing with sticks,
one whacked his mate, then there were six.
Six skating elephants learning how to drive,
one crashed, then there were five.
Five skating elephants heading for the door,
one didn't make it, then there were four.
Four skating elephants having a cup of tea,
one burnt his tongue, then there were three.
Three skating elephants all in a queue,
one stormed out, then there were two.
Two skating elephants singing a song,
one went out of tune , then there was one.
One skating elephant playing with his drum,
he accidentally broke it, then there were none.

Ben Ellwood (10)
Millbrook Primary School

Ten Flapping Chickens

Ten flapping chickens in the stomach of mine,
one stayed in, then there were nine.
Nine flapping chickens on a date,
one left, then there were eight.
Eight flapping chickens trying to get to heaven,
one broke her wing, then there were seven.
Seven flapping chickens trying to move bricks,
one broke her wing, then there were six.
Six flapping chickens learning how to dive,
one missed the water, then there were five.
Five flapping chickens going through the door,
one got squashed, then there were four.
Four flapping chickens sitting on a tree,
one fell off, then there were three.
Three flapping chickens trying to go, 'Cock-a-doodle-doo,'
one hurt her lungs, then there were two.
Two flapping chickens acting really dumb,
one banged into a cat, then there was one.
One flapping chicken basking in the sun,
then she got baked, then there were none.

James Burridge (9)
Millbrook Primary School

Ten Mad Monkeys

Ten mad monkeys hanging from a vine,
one dropped off and broke his leg, then there were nine.
Nine mad monkeys going to be late,
one got caught, then there were eight.
Eight mad monkeys travelling to Devon,
one slipped off the trees, then there were seven.
Seven mad monkeys doing plate tricks,
one knocked his head, then there were six.
Six mad monkeys about to dive,
one jumped into the water, then there were five.

Five mad monkeys beginning to be poor,
one died of starvation, then there were four.
Four mad monkeys eating lots of brie,
one ate too much, then there were three.
Three mad monkeys going to the loo,
one tripped in, then there were two.
Two mad monkeys weighed half a ton,
one dozed asleep then there was one.
One mad monkey eating delicious buns,
he ate too much, then there were none.

George Talbot (9)
Millbrook Primary School

TEN MISCHIEVOUS MONKEYS

Ten mischievous monkeys sitting all in line,
One went off to go to bed, then there were nine.
Nine mischievous monkeys, bananas they all ate,
One went all dizzy inside, then there were eight.
Eight mischievous monkeys, thinking they're in heaven,
One fell out of the tree, then there were seven.
Seven mischievous monkeys being a bunch of twits,
One got kidnapped by a man, then there were six.
Six mischievous monkeys taking great big dives,
One over did it a bit, then there were five.
Five mischievous monkeys laughing on the floor,
One got stung and hurt himself, then there were four.
Four mischievous monkeys playing by a tree,
One needed to go to the loo, then there were three,
Three mischievous monkeys trying on a shoe,
One got eaten by a tiger, then there were two.
Two mischievous monkeys wondering where the others had gone,
One went off to find them then there was one.
One mischievous monkey stood there all alone,
He collapsed with fear, then there were none.

Luke Stone (10)
Millbrook Primary School

I AM A DOLPHIN

I am a dolphin
I live in the sea
I was caught in a fishing net
for my gleaming fins you see.
I don't want my fins chopped off you know,
just a life with my family in my home.
So far it is horrible, there're no fish for my tea,
but a net over my dried up body.
My teeth are like dead blocks of cold ice
and my lips are like humps of stone.
A fearsome life for me,
no wonder I'm here, stuck in a net.
I'm surely going to die.
Before they come to kill me
I will close my eyes.
Here comes the fisherman, ready with his knife,
raising the knife in his hands.
My life is over, my fins are gone,
so he then chucks me in the sea.
I lie dead on the seabed.

Eleanor Middlebrook (10)
Millbrook Primary School

TEN PRANCING PIGS

Ten prancing pigs dancing in time,
One falls over, then there are nine.
Nine prancing pigs rushing through the gate,
One gets caught and then there are eight.
Eight prancing pigs on their way to Devon,
One gets lost and then there are seven.
Seven prancing pigs playing with sticks,
One hurts himself and then there are six.
Six prancing pigs waiting to dive,
One slips up, then there are five.

Five prancing pigs breaking the law,
One gets caught, then there are four.
Four prancing pigs climbing up a tree,
One falls out, then there are three.
Three prancing pigs wanting to go to the loo,
One gets locked in and then there are two.
Two prancing pigs having fun,
One falls off the equipment, then there is one.
One prancing pig eats a bun,
He daydreams and then there are none.

Joshua Preston (9)
Millbrook Primary School

TEN BALLISTIC LUNATICS

Ten ballistic lunatics singing in a rhyme,
One got nervous and rocketed off, then there were nine.
Nine ballistic lunatics building on a gate,
One got hit with a brick, then there were eight.
Eight ballistic lunatics flying around in heaven,
One fell through the clouds, then there were seven.
Seven ballistic lunatics baking an oven mix,
One fainted because of the smell, then there were six.
Six ballistic lunatics jumping around alive,
One slipped and broke his leg, then there were five.
Five ballistic lunatics playing on the seashore,
One tripped and drowned in the water, then there were four.
Four ballistic lunatics poking with a key,
One poked one in the eye, then there were three
Three ballistic lunatics running with a shoe,
One kicked one, then there were two.
Two ballistic lunatics eating a bun,
One ate one too many, then there was one.
One ballistic lunatic jogging around the garden for fun,
Then he booked a flight, off he went, then there were none.

Bradley Barefoot (9)
Millbrook Primary School

I Am A Dog

I am a dog,
I live in a kennel,
every day I'm locked up there.

I used to run around in the garden all day
chasing the flies in the sun.
I want to be free but no one can see me
all lonely in my dirty kennel.

I am a dog,
I live in a kennel,
every day I'm locked up in there.

I miss paddling in the pond,
splashing my way around the beautiful lily pads.
I want to be free but no one can see me
all lonely in my dirty kennel.

I am a dog,
I live in a kennel,
every day I'm lock up in there.

Why can't you just let me free?

Emma Joyce (10)
Millbrook Primary School

3.00 Friday

3.00 Friday, home at last,
I'm going to forget the week that's passed.
On Monday they stole my glasses
and hid them in one of the classes.
On Tuesday in games,
they kicked me and called me names.

On Wednesday Miss kept me in,
because they didn't throw their apples in the bin.
On Thursday they swore at me because of the test,
'cause mine was better than the rest.
3.00 Friday, I'm free, free, free!
For two days they can't get me.

Grace Keen (9)
Millbrook Primary School

THE LUCKLESS ELEPHANT

I am an elephant
And I miss my wild freedom,
I'd amble around
That lawless kingdom.

With all the other elephants
I'd have lots of baths,
In the land of the uncultivated jungle,
Where there are no rickety paths.

I am an elephant
And I miss my wild freedom,
I'd amble around
That lawless kingdom.

I miss the fabulous fund,
I miss the great days,
I miss the water
That Father shot at me in the best May.

I am an elephant, as soft as could be
And all I want is . . . to be free!

Andy Rogers (10)
Millbrook Primary School

TEN MAD PEOPLE

Ten mad people rushing in a line,
one trips over, then there were nine.
Nine mad people late for their dates,
one got lost, then there were eight.
Eight mad people waiting to go to heaven,
one died early, then there were seven.
Seven mad people getting in a mix,
one trips over, gets confused, then there were six.
Six mad people standing by a beehive,
one got stung, then there were five.
Five mad people waiting by a door,
somebody opens it, then there were four.
Four mad people shopping for free,
one had to pay, then there were three.
Three mad people looking at their shoes,
one didn't like his, then there were two.
Two mad people adding up a sum,
one couldn't add, then there was one.
One mad person talking to a nun,
he got chatted up then there were none.
No mad people left to rhyme,
so I guess that's it till next time.

Jamie Parsons (9)
Millbrook Primary School

3.10 FRIDAY

3.10 Friday, finished at last,
the nightmare is over, it's finally passed.
On Monday they flattened my food in the sink,
so all I had left was my water to drink.
On Tuesday they ripped the best page out of my book,
I found it with the felt pens that they took.

On Wednesday they trampled all over my work,
the other kids laughed and call me a jerk.
On Thursday they took all the money I had,
it made me dead cross but mainly sad.

3.10 Friday, finished at last
the nightmare is over, it's finally passed.

Lydia Preece (10)
Millbrook Primary School

I Am A Lion

I am a lion,
I live in a stuffy cage.
I can't stand it,
Everyone looks at me.

I used to pounce with my charming family,
No I plod around all on my own.
I want to be free!

I miss the lovely delicious meals
I used to have.
Now I can't eat
Because it's so bad.

If I was out I would
Bite,
Bite,
Bite,
You!

Don't you understand, I want to be free!

Laura Pryde (9)
Millbrook Primary School

The Yellow Spy

Yellow takes many forms,
In the sun, seaside and river.
It's in the wallpaper, in the dorms,
Its colour makes you shiver.

It gleams and glints in the silence
Of the moonlit sky.
The imposter's in the dorm, hence,
He is a spy.

His gun is shiny yellow
And his hat was rather mellow,
The destroyer of the peace,
His actions will now cease.

William Fotherby (11)
Moulsford School

Churches

A hymn singer,
A bell ringer,
A candle burner,
A religion learner.
A music player,
A silent prayer.
A vicar trainer,
A knowledge gainer.
A couple maker,
A grave staker.

With doors of birch, I am a church.

Max Edwards, Henry Gibbs (10) & Ben Gardner (11)
Moulsford School

FIRE!

A wood burner,
A warmth giver,
A spit turner,
A fiery river.

An ice melter,
A marshmallow toaster,
A heated shelter,
A pork roaster.

A charcoal maker,
A water boiler,
A life taker,
A rain foiler.

I burn many pyres,
For I am all fires.

Nicholas Phillips & Geoff Penington (10)
Moulsford School

THE MOULSFORD CAT

Marmaduke, the Moulsford cat,
He's been here a long time.
His eyes are green and piercing,
The colour of a lime.
He rids the school of mice,
There never was a rat.
But he's still warm and friendly,
He is the Moulsford cat!

Tom Dethridge (11)
Moulsford School

CHRISTMAS TIME

While the children are snoozing in their beds,
They have lovely Christmas thoughts in their heads.
They leave out lovely treats for Santa.
They are too excited to sleep,
Hoping that they will get wonderful toys to keep.
While they try to sleep,
They try not to peep.
So they squeeze their eyes tight, tight
But cannot do it, though they try and try.
But it's no good.
They can already hear Santa coming.
But it is just their mum coming to bed.
Then Santa is here and all the boys and girls
Wake bright and early to rush for their toys.

Chloe Dallimore
North Hinksey Primary School

THE RUSTLING AND BUSTLING

Out of the city where it was bustling
Into the woods where it was rustling
Trees swaying side to side
Bushes rustling, trees blustering
Wolves howling, cats prowling
Cold winds blow as quick as mice
Leaving leaves as cold as ice
Making my path narrower and narrower
Getting wetter and wetter
Making me shiver
When I got out, trembling and freezing, I shouted,
'Help!'

Adam Newport (8)
North Hinksey Primary School

A Truly Wonderful World For Me

Chocolate bars wherever you go,
Rain turns into flurries of snow,
My favourite programme, always on telly,
Lots and lots of ice cream and jelly.

Game Boy games only cost 2p,
My brother's always nice to me,
Have a mansion to myself,
Lots of toys up on my shelf.

Daddy lets me have some dogs,
Nasty people turn into frogs,
Allowed to stay up very late,
Can leave my sprouts upon my plate!

Home clothes every day at school,
My own private swimming pool,
All of this would certainly be,
A truly wonderful world for me.

Jessica Ryan (8)
Rupert House School

Rainbow

Red cheeks all rosy
Orange orange juice
Yellow daffodils in a posy
Green vegetables on the loose
Blue sky on the lake
Indigo as the night
Violet as the grape
A rainbow shining bright.

Milly Belcher (8)
Rupert House School

THE ANIMAL ARK

The beetles dart across the drive,
The bees buzz into their hive.

The hummingbirds hum in the tree,
The cats miaow for their tea.

The rabbits eat and leap about,
The hamsters are filling up their pouch.

The dogs are waiting for a walk,
The parrots make an awful squawk.

The sheep and cows baa and moo,
The monkeys jump with the kangaroos.

The fish swim in the sunlit seas,
The horses gallop in the breeze.

The ants work very hard,
The chickens peck grain in the yard.

The donkeys sleep, (they need a nap)
The mice are dancing with the rats.

Above me soars the singing lark,
That's the end of my animal ark!

Laura Wheatley (10)
Rupert House School

HORSES

Horses come in different sizes,
Some are scruffy, some win prizes.
Dudley is the horse that I ride.
In the winter he shelters inside.

Falabellas are the smallest.
The heavy Shires are the tallest.
I like it best when I ride bareback,
In the woods and along the track.

Sarah Innes (8)
Rupert House School

FAIRIES

I was sitting in my garden,
Under the pear tree,
When this bright spark
Floated up to me.

The spark was very pretty,
It had tiny little wings,
It danced upon my hand
And then it started to sing.

The spark was a fairy,
All pink and blue and red,
It had a head-dress of flowers,
Around its little head.

I asked the lovely fairy,
'What are you doing here?'
She danced up to me
And whispered in my ear.

'You an have one wish,
What would you like it to be?'
'I wish for a big mansion,
On an island in the sea!'

Sophia Lerche-Thomsen (9)
Rupert House School

DANGEROUS PETS

I have three tigers,
They are so cute,
I have one scorpion
And he's minute!

My killer whale's black,
My shark is white,
I hear them splashing
In the night!

My black widow spider's
Really sweet,
It has pink patches
On its feet!

My little cobra
Loves to spit!
I like to pat it
Quite a bit!

My vampire bat
Makes me smile,
He plays with my
Pet crocodile!

My six piranhas
Love to swim
And bite each other's
Shiny fins.

My pack of wolves
Keep me awake,
The hippos make
The whole house shake!

I love to keep
This lovely zoo,
But don't hug them
Or they'll kill you!

Olivia Barton
Rupert House School

The Blue Flamingo

As I was walking along one day,
A flock of flamingos got in my way,
They were all pink but one was blue,
Apparently her name was Sue.

I said hi and she said squawk,
I should have known she could not talk,
All the others had flown away,
But Sue just seemed to want to stay.

I liked her a lot and said so too,
She's really pretty and fluffy and blue,
Oh, she's so lovely I love her so much,
Her pale feathers are soft to touch.

I have to go home to go to bed,
I stroked her softly and patted her head,
I said goodbye to my blue friend
And now my poem is at its end.

Alice Buys (9)
Rupert House School

WHY CAN'T PARENTS?

Why can't parents be hip and cool
And buy us sweets for after school?
Why can't we choose what to wear?
Why can't we style and cut our hair?

Why can't we stay up really late,
Instead of going to bed at eight?
Why can't my parents give me pay?
Why can't I watch TV all day?

Why can't I have designer clothes?
Why can't I sniff and pick my nose?
Why can't I blow bubbles in my drink?
Why can't my school clothes be bright pink?

Why can't I eat burgers all day long?
I'm always right, you're always wrong!
Why can't I chew my food out loud?
Why is spitting not allowed?

Why can't my parents be on time?
Why can't I have a glass of wine?
Why can't I drive a flashy car?
Why can't they treat me like a star?

But my parents love me so,
More than I will ever know
And I love them, it's plain to see,
We are a happy family!

Sophie McDowell (10)
Rupert House School

My Granny

My old granny
Is so cool,
She even has
A swimming pool!

She never tells me
What to do,
Her funky clothes
Are always new.

She can dance
So very well,
How she does it
I can't tell.

She is the best,
I love her so,
All around her
Is a glow.

She takes me out
To different places,
We always meet
These bright new faces.

I love her lots,
She's the best, really,
She's so cool,
I love her dearly.

Penny Hall (9)
Rupert House School

SUN

Sun, you are so beautiful
Everyone should know
Every day you come to see us
And you really glow

Sun, you are so glorious
You stay up in the sky
Every night you go away
When the moon floats by

Sun, you are so happy
You really like to shine
You're very bright and yellow
You sparkle all the time

Sun, you are so wonderful
You make the moon shine bright
We see you up in the sky
You disappear at night.

Katie Halfhead (9)
Rupert House School

GREEN

Green grass,
Green leaves,
Green frogs,
Green trees.

Green books,
Green cheese,
Green eyes,
Green peas,
Why so much green?

Alex Bucknall (9)
Rupert House School

Seasons Of The Year

It is spring and the buds are out,
Then it's summer with sunshine of gold,
Autumn's getting ready for winter,
Now winter is here and it's cold.

Spring is back with fields full of lambs,
Summer's back with babies in prams,
Autumn's returned and cooler winds blow
And winter has come, bringing the snow.

Spring is full of palest green,
Summer has a golden sheen,
Autumn has colours of orange and red,
Winter is icy, the world looks dead.

Octavia Kerr (9)
Rupert House School

Tidying Up My Bedroom

My bedroom is a bombsite,
The cupboard doors won't close,
My homework's strewn all over the floor
And the sofa's lost its throws.

My bedroom is a pigsty,
I cannot reach my bed,
There's no room to put anything,
I need the garden shed.

My bedroom is now gleaming,
You can get in through the door,
I've accomplished the impossible,
I've tided up the floor!

Emily Binning (11)
Rupert House School

Why?

All day it rains,
Rain falling in sheets,
Warning that the world
Is finally ending.

Our lives, ending,
With the Earth that we've slowly destroyed,
With global warming
And mass destruction.

Why do we fight between nations?
Why the lust to kill our peers?
Why do we destroy God's creations?
Why, I ask you, why?

Emily Granger (11)
Rupert House School

Meeting An Alien

Why have you got three arms?
What's happened to your eye?
Why is your hair bright purple?
Have you used hair dye?

Your hair is so bright purple,
That it's glowing in the dark!
Your laser eyes are shining
And your teeth are like a shark!

Oh no! You are an alien!
I hope you won't eat me,
What about a milkshake?
I'll invite you round to tea!

Victoria Bushnell (9)
Rupert House School

JUNGLE

Tigers are prowling around,
Monkeys are swinging from the trees,
Beetles are crawling on the ground,
I can hear buzzing bees.

The parrots are screeching and squawking,
Black and red snakes are hissing,
Dark tribesmen are hunting and talking,
The monkeys are going missing.

The butterflies flap in the sky,
Soldier ants are crawling around,
Baby parrots are learning to fly,
The leopards do not make a sound.

Rebecca Roddan (8)
Rupert House School

ANIMALS

Dogs are sweet,
Hamsters are funny,
Birds go tweet,
I wish I had a bunny!

Hedgehogs are shy,
Bears are furry,
Crocodiles cry,
Cats are purry.

Snakes are slimy,
Orang-utans are hairy,
A horse's cot's shiny,
Spiders are scary!

Magdalena Case (8)
Rupert House School

Bonfire Night

Twisting, turning in the sky,
Up and up the sparks will fly.
Colours blending in the night,
Against the golden stars so bright.
Light the bonfire, flames will rise,
Steamy smoke up in the skies.
Stay up late at 11 o'clock,
Bang, bang, bang! Oh what a shock!
Red, yellow, blue and green,
It's the best display I've ever seen!
Rockets shoot up to the moon,
I can't wait to have the sparklers soon.
The 5th of November brings lots of joy,
To every adult, girl and boy!

Emma Ford (9)
Rupert House School

Sisters (Limericks)

My sister is a great big pain
It really is an awful shame.
She steals my toys
Then tells the boys
And I get all the blame!

She gets all sorts of things
That my grandma always brings.
As you can see
This annoys me
When she's in the shower, she sings!

Alice Barton (8)
Rupert House School

A Jungle Beastie

I was walking in a jungle on a jungle trail,
When I saw a jungle beastie
And I grabbed it by the tail
And the beastie took me to places
A man should never be,
He took me through trees,
He took me through bushes,
He took me to a clearing full of killer bees.
They stung me all over
And the beastie let out a howl
And dragged me to a river
And I took a breath as we went underwater.
I thought I would run out of breath
And this would be my death,
But the beastie came to shore,
Where the beastie and I departed.
I was walking in the jungle on a jungle trail,
Where I saw a jungle beastie with a long, long tail.

Milly Hibbert (9)
St Hugh's School, Carswell

Snowballs

Snowballs are fun,
Snowballs are soft,
You can throw them at each other,
Ice cream is cold just like snow,
You can play tennis with a tennis ball,
But not with a snowball.

Carolyn McClellan (7)
St Hugh's School, Carswell

WINTER

I hear robins chatting,
I hear fire cracking.

I taste snowflakes on my tongue,
I taste hot chocolate on my tongue.

I see snowmen and the whiteness of snow,
I see flames and the fire's glow.

I feel the coldness crunching when I walk,
I feel the warmth of my bed.

I smell the clear cold frost,
I smell the smoke of chimneys.

When I touch the snow,
When I touch the pillow

It is very soft.

Genevieve Bernard (7)
St Hugh's School, Carswell

WINTER DAYS

Short days, cold nights
Freezing ears and frostbite
Gardens bare, leafless trees
No sign of humming bees.

Chilly mornings, murky sky
Time for a hot mince pie
Howling winds, icy and bitter
Look at how the robins titter.

Lillie Owen (7)
St Hugh's School, Carswell

Harriet Of The Chariot Limerick

There once was a girl called Harriet
Who rode around in a chariot.
She had a pet dog
Who looked like a hog
And she was too lazy to carry it.

One day she sat in her chair
Combing her long brown hair.
She called for her maid
Who hadn't been paid
But Harriet didn't much care.

She wasn't fond of mice
And she didn't like rolling dice
She was cruel to her friends
Though her age was ten
So she wasn't particularly nice.

Dora Taylor (8)
St Hugh's School, Carswell

Snow

Today is a fun day,
Because it is now snowing,
So we're going out to play,
As snowdrifts are growing.

Shrieks and shouts as snowballs fly,
The grey heavy clouds in the sky,
I wonder when winter will end
And I have to say bye to my friend.

Peter Truran (8)
St Hugh's School, Carswell

Snowmen Haiku

Snowmen, fat, soggy
Giant, pudgy, snowy, fun
To knock down, snowmen!

William Barnes (7)
St Hugh's School, Carswell

Battleships

Battleships
float out
to sea
with millions
of machinery.
They fire
torpedoes
which race through the abyss
and hit
the enemy submarine.

Christopher Gray (7)
St Hugh's School, Carswell

Snow Haiku

Cold, frosty, chilly
Clear, dull, seems to always be
There. Cold, icy snow.

Harry Sayer (8)
St Hugh's School, Carswell

Vegetables

Ucky, sticky vegetables all slimy on your plate.
The way your mother yells at you to make you eat all eight.
Shrivelled, crunchy cauliflower and broccoli
That's a week out of date!
It leaves me in quite a dreadful state!

Philippa Coull (8)
St Hugh's School, Carswell

Ice

Ice,
Fun, slippery,
Dangerous, clear, icy
Fun to skate on
Ice.

Bethan Elliott (8)
St Hugh's School, Carswell

Jumbo Dance

Once an elephant did ballet,
Was he good? No way!
He tripped and stumbled and fell around,
He was rather dangerous,
His teacher found!

Emma Mackilligin (8)
St Hugh's School, Carswell

THE GARDEN IN WINTER

Through the snowy window,
I heard a chirping robin,
Above the trees, the falling snow
glistened on the rooftops,
Delicious icing sugar,
Chimneys sparkle.
Below the eaves the icicles hang
like luscious ice cream cones.
The owl hoots at night when the moon is bright.
In the garden the frigid snowmen
might throw snowballs at me.
This is no bleak mid winter!

Cameron Cockburn (7)
St Hugh's School, Carswell

WATER SIMILES

Icy cold water feels like the sharp edge of a knife,
cutting crunchy pork crackling.
Falling water sounds like
a clashing war with smacking swords.
Spring water smells like
a perfumed bath on a balmy evening.
Saltwater tastes like
a slimy Brussels sprout on your plate.
Still water looks like
a worn marble mosaic shining on a Roman ruin.

Calum Cockburn (9)
St Hugh's School, Carswell

THE FINAL

Here comes Shearer
Here comes Speed
Here comes Bellamy
It's the Newcastle team.

On to the pitch
It's so great
They never lose
Well that's what Man U hate.

Here comes Beckham
Here comes Keane
They're so rubbish
It's the Man U team.

The game kicks off
It begins to start
Bellamy goes forward
As fast as a dart.

The whistle goes
It's half-time
It's extremely loud
On Tyneside.

The crowd are loving it
It's great what they've seen
Bellamy breaks through
Hang on, it's in.
The whistle goes
They didn't slip up
It's so fantastic
They've won the cup!

Sam Edmonds (10)
West Kidlington Primary School

The Big Match

On to the pitch ran every man,
The ref blew his whistle and the game began,
Each and every player taking lots of time and care,
One threw a header and it messed up his hair,
As the muddy brown ball soared into the net,
People in the crowd wondered how many goals will they get.

Happily the cheerful players trooped back onto their half,
One stumbled which made the ref laugh,
Then the loosing team threw a ferocious fowl,
Which resulted in an awfully nasty row!
They thought it was yellow, but it was red,
The fouled man was angry, now with a graze on his head.

The home team it was winning now,
The score was 3-2, with just a minute left,
The victory was true, but suddenly,
The referee was pointing to the spot!

A very unfair penalty, our team could lose the lot,
The ball was placed, the man retired
And turned to make his run
And everybody held their breath,
Until the deed was done.

The ball went fast: the ball was hard,
Between the bar and post
And all the crowd thought all was lost,
The thing they feared the most.
But then to everyone's surprise and everyone's delight,
The goalie moved as if on springs
And like a man in flight.

He touched the ball and tripped it wide
And cheers burst round the ground
And in the noise they hardly heard
The final whistle sound.

Freddie Roberts (10)
West Kidlington Primary School

Dreams

I had a dream,
It was quite extreme;
I flew through the air,
As the wind blew past my hair,
When I looked down below
The ground was covered with snow.

It began to get dark,
The lights were on in the park,
As I blinked
I began to think;

The sun went down
Without a frown,
Although I whispered to myself;
Out of my mouth:
Carry on Emma.

The next morning came
And the sun rose
With a little pose
I told myself: *go home*
That was my dream!

Emma Trafford (10)
West Kidlington Primary School

THE LADY ON THE STAIR

The lady on the stair,
She never goes,
She's always there.

The lady on the stair,
The only work,
To calm her head,
Does not move her,
She's almost dead.

The lady on the stair,
She never runs or jumps or skips,
She either lies there,
Or;
She sits.

The lady on the stair,
The little stray,
Closer up than right down there,
Vanishes still;
But far away.

The lady on the stair,
Her life a grey cloud above a grey bear,
The face of her; it is not fair,
Will she go, just not be there?

The lady on the stair,
As I know: she does not belong,
But to get away: she would not dare,
For she is a lady of great song,
Or she is the lady on the stair.

The lady on the stair,
She never goes,
She's always there.

Isabel Taylor (11)
West Kidlington Primary School

Kitty's Dream

As I settle in my master's chair
A large bowl of fish is in my head,
I drift of sleeping in my seat
Calmly, calmly in my new-found bed.

Fishes darting in and out,
As I sleep silently in this chair,
Scampering feet of little mice galore,
Whilst birds fly swiftly in the air.

I reach out a soft little paw,
Why can't I reach that tasty dish
Of sweet, succulent fish?

It's true, it's true,
I hear it I do,
That wonderful sound of a tin and a spoon.

Clatter, clink, clitter, clash!
Jump run, quick, quick
I hear it, I hear it!
Oh no look out . . . *smash!*

I'm frozen to the ground,
Uh oh, run, hide!
Too late he's here at my side,
I look up at my master's angry frown,
Then again back at the ground.

Before I know it out in the cold,
Whimper, whimper let me in!
Whilst from inside come a few muffled sounds,
Then *click, click, click.*

I quickly awake with a jump,
Oh no, look at what I've done,
A hole in my master's brand new chair!

Georgia Jones (11)
West Kidlington Primary School

ENVIRONMENT CRISIS

Away from the city, far from the town
A little cat lies there on the ground.
Helplessly begging for some food,
Been excluded from the group.
At the smelly, dirty dump,
An old dog in a slump,
The scraggy rag, rummaging in the mess.
Then smells something yummy but it's just an old dress.
In the gloomy woods, away from the stares,
A tiny mouse glares at something.
Then starts munching,
Trying to find some kind of shelter.
Under the filthy earth,
One little rabbit lay,
Trying to get some warmth in bits of grimy hay.
Wanting her mother to come back with its feed,
Some old, scraggy bits of weed came back.
As you can see, natural, living things
Can end up in the confusing world.

Rebecca Washington (10)
West Kidlington Primary School

IN THE JUNGLE

Today I went to a jungle,
To find the monkeys swinging from tree,
To see the slippy snakes slither
And to feel heat of hot, hot sun.

I saw the gorillas rumble,
I saw the birds tweet, tweet,
To find a chimpanzee eating his tea
And to feel the heat of hot, hot sun.

I saw an Indian tribe,
I felt the hard brushed leaves,
I tasted the soft sweet air,
Today I went to a jungle.

Jack Emmings (10)
West Kidlington Primary School

Creepy-Crawlies

Creepy-crawlies on the wall and stair,
Creepy-crawlies on the dining room chairs.
Creepy-crawlies in the butler's hair,
Creepy-crawlies flying in the air.

Crawling into Dad's best suit,
Climbing up Mum's old gardening boot.
Crouching in the purse and nibbling the loot,
Creeping down the trouser leg and onto the foot.

Relaxing in the middle of Fred's new book,
Rummaging around the moustache of the cook.
Racing amongst the coats on the hook,
Running through the laundry without a second look.

Longing for a piece of delicious chocolate nest,
Leaping over the sweatiest vest.
Laughing at the funny plump guests,
Longing for the evening dress (one of the best).

Spoiling the scoop of ice cream and all the rest,
Spotting the sweets, just to be a pest.
Swimming in the butter is the ultimate test,
Sprawling over the iced cake till it's messed.

Sophie Proffitt (10)
West Kidlington Primary School

The Feelings World

The feelings world is full of calm,
A world ruled by care,
Love, peace and happiness, yes they all live there,
Blue sky all around,
Lighting up the spotless ground,

The clouds above are ghosts of white,
Who always dance through the night
And happiness is the playful one
And when it plays you can hear it say,
'I've brought you happiness today'.

All around constant peace never sound,
Birds singing happily all around
And all the feelings dance and shout
And even the animals prance about

And as the sun goes away,
It's the end of another fun day,
All the feelings say goodnight
And go to bed without a fright.

Lee Smith (10)
West Kidlington Primary School

The Story Of A Field

The fields were green
Best I've ever seen

With lots of bright grass
As shiny as glass

Trees swaying back and forth
Wind was blowing in the north

Dogs leaping in the air
Little children everywhere

Bikes making mud tracks
While people walk home with their macs.

Harry Taylor (11)
West Kidlington Primary School

EARTH

The space shuttle flew far and near
While men in pubs were drinking beer
Up in space was a beautiful place
The place that was there looked like a face.

Down on Earth, every second a new birth
Child after child, day after day
Some born in February some in May
Most of them able to play.

Now we come to the worst of all
That no one can ever change at all
Although this part might not sound so bad
For centuries to come people will get mad.

Crimes make people very sad
They also commit people to be bad
Some do not think to care
And most certainly don't like to share.

Here is the best of all
This Earth is really shaped like a ball
A ball that spins around the sun
With luck maybe to see someone!

Lee Sherlock (10)
West Kidlington Primary School

The Book Of Shadows

Opening the pages of the book,
You appear in a world
Where perched on every tree sits a rook
And at your feet lay magic pearls.

The sky is filled with shadows
And evil is about,
But over in the meadows,
Light shines straight out.

Bare trees try to grab at you,
Black bats cry out,
Shadows jump out at you,
Watch out for a bear's snout.

You can feel the anger everywhere,
You can almost touch it,
But be careful to look out there,
To look out for an *it.*

You hope you can get out soon,
It's like trying to jump a hurdle,
You feel like you're in a spoon,
Like you're going round in a circle.

A man appears in front of you,
Right in the middle of the meadows,
He walks right towards you,
But you come out of the Book of Shadows.

Ellis Wiggins (10)
West Kidlington Primary School

The Four Seasons

Autumn comes just once a year
And every time I stand, cheering,
The leaves *crunch* under your feet,
A rainbow of colours beneath you,
Frigid nights amaze you,
Although it's pleasant to get into bed!

Winter is the one that follows,
As icy cold winds whip up the leaves,
Up off the ice-bound floor,
The same as a fan blowing out of control,
For those who brave to go outside,
Remember your glove, scarves and hats!

Spring is the one that comes up next,
The season of new bright,
Lambs are born, cute and fluffy,
Daffodils comes out bright and beautiful,
It starts becoming light,
Like a new light bulb has been put in.

Now we're into summer,
The seasons everyone loves,
Bees buzz around without a care in the world,
Like fairies dotted in the sky,
There's going to be a sizzling sun,
So put on your sunscreen or you'll crisp!

Lauren Green (10)
West Kidlington Primary School

My Dream

Floating on the clouds,
Candyfloss all around,
Lollipops on the floor,
People but no sound.
Softness on my body,
Floating through the air,
Nothing on my skin,
No clothes as I am bare.
Unicorns dancing round me,
Round and round they go,
Their horns are glimmering in the moonlight,
Suddenly they all go.
Floating through the air again,
Angels touch my limbs,
Glitter all around me
And angels sing some hymns.
I am a silver star now,
Shooting through the night,
I am very very beautiful
And very very bright.
Now I am me again,
So I lay down on the clouds,
Baby angels tuck me in
And I go to sleep hearing no sounds.

Jodie Waddle (11)
West Kidlington Primary School

MY DOG JASPER

I once had a dog,
He had a shiny wet nose,
The most loveable dog
With a fear of the hose.

Sometimes at home,
He was silky and soft,
Tail always wagging,
His ears aloft.

When out for a walk,
Every puddle he would find,
The muddier the better,
The word rugby player sprung to mind.

To Nicholas and me
He was a great friend,
A stranger came near,
Our safety he would defend.

Beauty and friendship,
A special bond,
Loyalty and trust,
To which any child would respond.

Shannon Weston (10)
West Kidlington Primary School

IN A DREAM

In a dream;
A dream in time gone by,
Soaring over green, fluffy clouds,
I feel I can fly . . .
In time gone by.

In a dream;
A dream filled with beauty,
With all the flowers shooting up,
Soft and silky . . .
In time gone by.

In a dream;
A dream like no other,
All the magical angels,
Feel like brothers . . .
In time gone by.

In a dream;
A dream in the winter,
The snow is glistening,
Like the dew in the summer . . .
In time gone by.

In a dream;
A dream on a birthday,
At a party to celebrate . . .
A special day . . .
In time gone by.

In a dream;
A dream in time gone by,
Soaring over green, fluffy clouds,
I feel I can fly . . .
In time gone by.

Nicola Fairgrieve (10)
West Kidlington Primary School